Jim Burns's work represents his integrity, intelligence, and his heart for kids. The *Uncommon* high school group studies will change some lives and save many others.

stephen arterburn
Bestselling Author, *Every Man's Battle*

Jim Burns has found the right balance between learning God's Word and applying it to life. The topics are relevant, up to date and on target. Jim gets kids to think. This is a terrific series, and I highly recommend it.

les j. christie
Chair of Youth Ministry, William Jessup University, Rocklin, California

There are very few people in the world who know how to communicate life-changing truth effectively to teens. Jim Burns is one of the best. These studies are biblically sound, hands-on practical and just plain fun. This one gets a five-star endorsement.

ken davis
Author and Speaker (www.kendavis.com)

The practicing youth worker always needs more ammunition. The *Uncommon* high school group studies will get that blank stare off the s of the kids at your youth meeting!

jay kesler
President Emeritus, Taylor University, Upl

D1444042

In the *Uncommon* high school group studies, Jim Burns pulls together the key ingredients for an effective series. He captures the combination of teen involvement and a solid biblical perspective with topics that are relevant and straightforward. This will be a valuable tool in the local church.

dennis "tiger" mcluen
Executive Director, Youth Leadership (www.youthleadership.com)

Young people need the information necessary to make wise decisions related to everyday problems. The *Uncommon* high school group studies will help many young people integrate their faith into everyday life, which, after all, is our goal as youth workers.

miles mcpherson
Senior Pastor, The Rock Church, San Diego, California

This is a resource that is user-friendly, learner-centered and intentionally biblical. I love having a resource like this that I can recommend to youth ministry volunteers and professionals.

duffy robbins
Professor of Youth Ministry, Eastern University, St. Davids, Pennsylvania

The *Uncommon* high school group studies provide the motivation and information for leaders and the types of experience and content that will capture high school people. I recommend it highly.

denny rydberg
President, Young Life (www.younglife.org)

Jim Burns has done it again! This is a practical, timely and reality-based resource for equipping teens to live life in the fast-paced, pressure-packed adolescent world of today.

rich van pelt
President, Compassion International, Denver, Colorado

Jim Burns has his finger on the pulse of youth today. He understands their mindsets and has prepared these studies in a way that will capture their attention and lead them to greater maturity in Christ.

rick warren
Senior Pastor, Saddleback Church, Lake Forest, California
Author of *The Purpose Driven Life*

uncommon
be extraordinary.

high school group study

jim burns &
doug fields

general editors

spiritual gifts

Published by Gospel Light
Ventura, California, U.S.A.
www.gospellight.com
Printed in the U.S.A.

Opening devotions for units written by Jim Burns and Doug Fields. Opening devotions
for all sessions written by Joey O'Connor. Study questions written by Kate Bayless.

Library of Congress Cataloging-in-Publication Data
Burns, Jim.
Burns, Jim, 1953-
Uncommon Bible study series : spiritual gifts / Jim Burns and Doug Fields.
p. cm.
ISBN 978-0-8307-4645-3 (trade paper)
1. Gifts, Spiritual—Study and teaching. I. Fields, Doug, 1962- II. Title.
BT767.3.B87 2008
234'.13071—dc22
2008021892

Rights for publishing this book outside the U.S.A. or in non-English languages are
administered by Gospel Light Worldwide, an international not-for-profit ministry.
For additional information, please visit www.glww.org, email info@glww.org, or write
to Gospel Light Worldwide, 1957 Eastman Avenue, Ventura, CA 93003, U.S.A.

dedication

To South Coast Community Church and
First Presbyterian Church, Orange:

We were blessed to be together at two of the
greatest churches in the world. Your input and
influence on our lives have been eternally
transforming. We have now moved on to other
ministries, but we are deeply grateful for the
start that you gave us as well as the life-long
friendship and partnership we count as
one of the joys of our lives.

Jim Burns and Doug Fields

contents

how to use
the *uncommon*
group bible studies

Each *Uncommon* Group Bible Study contains 12 sessions, which are divided into 3 stand-alone units of 4 sessions each. You may choose to teach all 12 sessions consecutively, to use just one unit or to present individual sessions. You know your group, so do what works best for you and your students.

This is your leader's guidebook for teaching your group. Electronic files (in PDF format) of each session's student handouts are available for download at **www.gospellight.com/uncommon/spiritual_gifts.zip**. The handouts include the "message," "dig," "reflect" and "meditation" sections of each study, formatted for easy printing. You may print as many copies as you need for your group.

Each session opens with a devotional meditation written for you, the youth leader. As hectic and trying as youth work is much of the time, it's important never to neglect your interior life. Use the devotions to refocus your heart and prepare yourself to share with kids the message that has already taken root in you. Each of the 12 sessions are divided into the following sections:

starter
Young people will stay in your youth group if they feel comfortable and make friends in the group. This section is designed for you and the students to get to know each other better.

dig

Many young people are biblically illiterate. In this section, students will dig into the Word of God and will begin to interact on a personal level with the concepts.

reflect

The conclusion to the study will allow students to reflect on some of the issues presented in the study on a more personal level.

meditation

A closing Scripture for the students to read and reflect on.

unit I

spiritual gifts that demonstrate God's love and presence

In some ways, you might say that Doug and I (Jim) have grown up together. Actually, I'm nine years older, but we've "hung out" since 1977. I had hair in 1977, and Doug was a junior higher in my youth group who was still wondering if girls had "cooties," and his strongest love was baseball. My first remembrance of Doug Fields was that he was a very confident kid in our youth group who had the possibility of being a little obnoxious. I told him as an eighth-grader, "You will either end up in prison or be one of the most incredible youth workers in the twentieth century." Well, he hasn't made it to prison yet, and he is truly one of a handful of youth specialists leading the way into the twenty-first century.

God has truly gifted Doug with several outstanding abilities and talents. It has been one of the joys of my life to watch him be used by God to reach thousands of students and come alongside thousands of youth workers to make this world a better place. However, what has been perhaps the most exciting part of seeing God's hand in his life is the fact that he has searched out his spiritual gifts and is using them for the glory of God.

Doug came to me more than 10 years ago when we were working together at South Coast Community Church and suggested that we do a series on spiritual gifts for our high school group. He had been learning a great deal about his own spiritual gifts and thought it was time to have us share what we both had been learning with our kids.

He tested the Bible studies at Community Presbyterian Church in Danville, California, and we did a series at South Coast. Today, we would both say that helping students find their spiritual gifts is one of the highlights of our ministries. One such student was Kim Halloway, who came up to me after a session on the gift of hospitality and was so excited to discover that she definitely had been given the gift of hospitality. She realized that she had been using it without knowing it was a spiritual gift and said she would now actively use the gift of hospitality to serve God.

Helping students find their spiritual gifts and then helping them to use those gifts for the glory of God is what this study is all about. The first session is about discovery. In it, you have the opportunity to invite most of your students—probably for the first time—to discover the wonderful world of spiritual gifts. Your students will never be the same as you enlist them in God's army of grace-gifted people who demonstrate God's love and presence through their lives. Our prayer for this first section is that you will be able to develop relationships with your students like we did with each other two decades ago. Just as we've grown in our friendship, spiritual lives and our ministries, we believe you can have the same blessing from God with your students.

spiritual gifts: are they for everyone?

Now to him who is able to do immeasurably more than all we ask or imagine, according to his power that is at work within us, to him be glory in the church and in Christ Jesus throughout all generations, for ever and ever! Amen.

EPHESIANS 3:20-21

As you begin this exciting new Bible study on spiritual gifts, you may be asking the same question a lot of other youth workers occasionally ask: *Am I really using my spiritual gifts to their fullest potential?* Or you may be wondering about the same thing as the young people in your youth group: *What are spiritual gifts, and has God given me any?*

Our hope and prayer for you as you flip open the pages to these 12 lessons is that you walk away . . .

• **Encouraged:** It's so easy for youth workers to get discouraged by the lack of progress they see in their own lives and the lives of teenagers. God has gifted you, and He wants you to be encouraged in your ministry through the spiritual gifts He has given you. Be encouraged—God is with you today!

• **Empowered:** The Holy Spirit wants to use you in great ways for His kingdom. That's why you are empowered by the Holy Spirit to use your spiritual gifts to build up the Body of Christ. You are empowered by God!

• **Equipped:** Once you discover your spiritual gifts, it's critical to be equipped to use them in the lives of students and their families. God would never give you a spiritual gift without equipping you first.

Why not take some time to pray about what the Lord will do through this exciting process?

*But our all-wise God has apportioned His gifts as He wills,
and one day He will require from each of us an accounting of our
use of those gifts . . . if you and I really want to be used by our Lord,
it will pay us to ferret out what our particular ability is,
then get busy putting it to use.*

JEANETTE LOCKERBIE

spiritual gifts: are they for everyone?

starter

PERSONAL SURVEY: Fill in the following lines below.

Three things that I am good at:

1. _____
2. _____
3. _____

Three things that I am not so good at:

1. _____
2. _____
3. _____

Three things that I would like to try:

1. _____
2. _____
3. _____

Note: You can download this group study guide in 8$\frac{1}{2}$" x 11" format at **www.gospellight.com/uncommon/spiritual_gifts.zip.**

Three things that scare me:

1. _____
2. _____
3. _____

Three things that I would like to get better at:

1. _____
2. _____
3. _____

Three words that I would use to describe myself:

1. _____
2. _____
3. _____

dig

Whatever you do, work at it with all your heart, as working for the Lord, not for men, since you know that you will receive an inheritance from the Lord as a reward.

Colossians 3:23-24

1. What are spiritual gifts? What is their purpose? Write your definition of spiritual gifts below.

    _____
    _____
    _____
    _____
    _____
    _____
    _____

Spiritual gifts are an important piece of our personal relationship with Jesus Christ as well as a vital part of how we
interact with, support and grow with the Body of Christ.
We are all "fearfully and wonderfully made" (Psalm 139:14),
uniquely constructed by the Master Craftsman with the
perfect set of traits, abilities and talents. These gifts and
abilities are not for our own credit, but to bring God glory.

2. Spiritual gifts are discussed in four different passages in the
New Testament. Read the passage of Scripture listed below
and list the various gifts mentioned in that section.

Romans 12:6-8   1 Corinthians 12:4-11;
                                        1 Corinthians 12:28-30

1. _____   1. _____

2. _____   2. _____

3. _____   3. _____

4. _____   4. _____

5. _____   5. _____

6. _____   6. _____

7. _____   7. _____

                                        8. _____

                                        9. _____

                                       10. _____

Ephesians 4:7-8,11-12   1 Peter 4:9-11

1. _____   1. _____

2. _____   2. _____

3. _____   3. _____

4. _____

5. _____

3. Look at the complete list on the previous page. What do you
    notice about the kinds of spiritual gifts on this list?

    ....

    ....

    ....

    ....

    ....

They are called *gifts* for two reasons: first because we received
them from the Holy Spirit, and second because they are all
meant to be used to assist and aid the Body of Christ. We received these spiritual gifts, but we also must learn how to
utilize them and give them away.

4. Do you think some gifts are more important than others?

    ....

    ....

    ....

    ....

    ....

5. Read Romans 12:6-8. According to this passage, if you have
    a particular gift, what should you do?

    ....

    ....

    ....

    ....

    ....

6. First Corinthians 12:1 says, "Now concerning spiritual gifts, brethren, I do not want you to be uninformed" (*RSV*). Continue reading verses 4 to 6. What point does Paul want to make clear about spiritual gifts?

7. Read 1 Corinthians 12:12-26. What does Paul's metaphor in these verses say about the importance of and connection between the various spiritual gifts?

8. Read and summarize 1 Peter 4:10. Explain how your specific gifts are to be used.

9. How do spiritual gifts benefit others and also accomplish God's work?

_____

_____

_____

_____

_____

_____

discovering your gifts

Do you know what spiritual gifts you have? While no single person except Jesus Christ possesses all spiritual gifts, all Christians have at least one spiritual gift. So how do you find out what yours is? Here are some suggestions for discovering what your spiritual gifts may be.

try it

Sometimes the only way to know if God has gifted you in a certain area is to try out the gift. You will never know if you have the gift of teaching unless you try to teach! Look at the list of spiritual gifts and think back over the last few months.

1. What is one gift that you have recently tried out, and how did the experience work out?

_____

_____

_____

_____

_____

2. Again, looking at your list, what is one spiritual gift that you would be interested in trying out during the upcoming week?

....

....

....

....

....

....

3. Brainstorm an opportunity that you could have to put this gift into action.

....

....

....

....

....

....

examine your feelings

Your feelings can be good indicators of where your gifts lie. If you experiment with the gift of teaching and feel extremely uncomfortable and embarrassed, then perhaps you don't have the gift (at this time).

On the other hand, if you were to experiment with the gift of hospitality and find that you enjoy entertaining people, sheltering them and feeding needy neighbors, then you most likely have the gift of hospitality.

1. Do you like being a leader? Do you enjoy helping others? Do you crave knowledge and wisdom? Which of the spiritual gifts do you enjoy doing?

    _____

    _____

    _____

    _____

    _____

    _____

2. Which spiritual gifts are less enjoyable for you?

    _____

    _____

    _____

    _____

    _____

    _____

3. Remember that just because you find something difficult or unpleasant doesn't necessarily mean that you don't have the spiritual gift! Read Exodus 3:7-13. In these verses, God is calling Moses up to be a leader. What is Moses' response?

    _____

    _____

    _____

    _____

    _____

    _____

4. What is God's response?

_____

_____

_____

_____

_____

_____

ask those around you

Often times, God will use other Christians in your life to reveal His will to you. Although it may be difficult for you to see your own gifts, those around you may have a clearer perspective about your gifts and talents.

1. If you feel comfortable, ask some of your friends and peers what spiritual gifts they see exhibited in your life. List those gifts below.

_____

_____

_____

_____

_____

2. Did your friends' and peers' responses surprise you in any way? Why or why not?

_____

_____

_____

_____

_____

_____

look for opportunities

Another way that God can reveal His will to you is through your circumstances. Do opportunities for hospitality keep knocking at your door? Are you continually presented with chances for leadership? God may be providing opportunities for your spiritual gifts to be revealed.

1. In the last few months, which of the following spiritual gifts have you had opportunities to use?

    Spiritual Gift   Opportunity

    _____   _____

    _____   _____

    _____   _____

    _____   _____

    _____   _____

2. Did you use those gifts? What happened in the situation when you did?

    _____

    _____

    _____

    _____

    _____

Remember to be open to the Holy Spirit surprising you with gifts outside of your normal operating range. You may have one set of gifts at this point in your life, but down the road, those gifts may change according to how the Holy Spirit directs.

using your gifts

So . . . how do you know if you are using your particular spiritual gifts to the glory of God?

evaluate your effectiveness

Occasionally, stop and think about if you are being effective in the role you are in. Ask yourself these three questions:

1. *Am I being effective?*
2. *Am I having a worthwhile impact on the people I am serving?*
3. *Is God using me in this particular area?*

Have you ever been involved in a ministry where you felt ineffective? What do you think was the cause?

_____

_____

_____

_____

_____

_____

_____

_____

There are various reasons why you might not be effective in a particular role. It may be that you were not given that specific spiritual gift, or it may be that you are not giving the task the attention and effort it requires.

expect confirmation from the body of Christ
Often times, God will use other Christians in your life to give you guidance and direction. Fellow believers should be encouraging and discouraging you (with love) in what you do. Listen to them, value their perspective, and then weigh their comments in prayerful consideration.

Who in your life can you trust to provide insight and guidance about your spiritual gifts?

_____

_____

_____

_____

_____

_____

failing to use God's gifts
But what happens if we don't use the spiritual gifts that God has bestowed on us?

we bring displeasure to God
In Matthew 25, Jesus tells the Parable of the Talents in which a man entrusted three of his servants with sums of money. Two of the servants invested the money, earning more than the master had originally given them. When the master returned, he said to each of them, "Well done, good and faithful servant. You have been faithful with a few things; I will put you in charge of many things" (Matthew 25:21). However, when the third servant came before the master, he said, "I knew you were a hard man . . . so

I was afraid and went out and hid your talent in the ground. See, here is what belongs to you" (vv. 24-25).

Read Matthew 25:26-30. What was the master's response to the third servant?

_____

_____

_____

_____

_____

Although in this passage, a talent refers to a sum of money—worth more than one thousand dollars in today's money—our understanding of a talent (a gift or ability) also applies in this parable. God has given us specific talents and abilities that He wants us to use—or we risk losing them.

we let down the body of Christ as a whole
"God has arranged the parts . . . just as he wanted them to be. If one part suffers, every part suffers with it" (1 Corinthians 12:18,26). What are the consequences if we don't use our gifts?

_____

_____

_____

_____

_____

reflect

1. What would happen to the Body of Christ if everyone had the same gifts?

   _____

   _____

   _____

   _____

   _____

   _____

2. Why is it important to discover your spiritual gifts?

   _____

   _____

   _____

   _____

   _____

3. What should you do if you have a friend who is not using his or her spiritual gift?

   _____

   _____

   _____

   _____

   _____

   _____

4. What spiritual gifts do you believe you currently have?

I believe that I have the gift of _____ because . . .

_____

_____

_____

I believe that I have the gift of _____ because . . .

_____

_____

_____

I believe that I have the gift of _____ because . . .

_____

_____

_____

5. What spiritual gifts are you fairly certain that you do not possess? List the reasons why you feel you don't have these gifts below.

_____

_____

_____

_____

_____

6. Are you currently using your spiritual gifts? If not, where do you sense God calling you to use your spiritual gifts?

_____

_____

_____

_____

_____

7. How can understanding your own spiritual gifts help you within your family? In your youth group? In your church?

_____

_____

_____

_____

_____

_____

_____

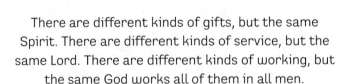

meditation

There are different kinds of gifts, but the same
Spirit. There are different kinds of service, but the
same Lord. There are different kinds of working, but
the same God works all of them in all men.

1 CORINTHIANS 12:4-6

discovering the right path

the gift of wisdom and the gift of knowledge

He who walks with the wise grows wise,
but a companion of fools suffers harm.

PROVERBS 13:20

As Christians and youth workers, we all need youth ministry mentors. Each one of us has struggled at one time or another with disillusionment, frustration or confusion in our ministries—or maybe we just needed some practical advice on how to help a teenager in need. Regardless of the situation, we all need someone whom we can call to talk through the issues we are having and bring clarity to our circumstances.

Who is your youth ministry mentor? Who gives you spiritual input and advice? Who listens to you about your struggles and questions? Who do you admire for his or her faithfulness and hungry desire to know God in a deeper and more meaningful way? God has not designed youth ministry to be a solitary, lonely experience. He wants you to walk with the wise so that you can grow wise. Coming alongside someone with more life experience, practical knowledge and spiritual insight is just what you and every youth worker needs to persevere in the ministry that God has called you to do.

If you don't have a youth ministry mentor, you need to find one. If you can't find someone who has youth ministry experience, find an older, wiser, knowledgeable brother or sister in Christ who will be in your corner to cheer you on. You can learn many lessons and avoid making many mistakes if you listen to someone who has walked the road before you.

Begin to pray today for God to direct you to someone who can listen, encourage and pray with you. God will use other people in extraordinary and divine ways to give you more wisdom and knowledge. And He will use you in extraordinary ways as well as you take the wisdom and pass it on to others.

Not only are we to ask God for wisdom, but we are to ask in faith. Someone has said, "Doubt is a non-conductor of grace." We are not to be double-minded, wanting partly our way and partly God's way.

MILLIE STAMM

discovering the right path

the gift of wisdom and the gift of knowledge

starter

TOPICAL TRIVIA: See if you can figure out the correct responses to the following trivia questions. (Answers can be found at the end of the study.)

1. Which popular trivia game is available in such editions as "Totally 80s," "Genius" and "Disney"?
2. What are the four books of the Bible that are known as "wisdom literature"?
3. Which word means someone who is all-knowing?
   a. omnipresent
   b. omniknowledgeable

      c. omnipotent

      d. omniscient

4. What Bible character is especially known for his wisdom?

5. What is the study of wisdom called?

6. What is the study of knowledge called?

dig

For to one is given the word of wisdom through the Spirit,
and to another the word of knowledge according to the same Spirit.

1 CORINTHIANS 12:8

Is it possible to have knowledge without wisdom? Is it possible to have wisdom without knowledge? In this study, we will examine two related but separate gifts mentioned in the Bible: the gift of wisdom and the gift of knowledge.

the gift of wisdom

Have you ever met a person you would label as "wise"? Some people just seem to have the ability to give solid counsel and good advice. These people likely have the gift of wisdom. Although the Bible challenges all of us to pursue wisdom, there are some people who have an exceptional ability to see clearly.

1. How would you describe wisdom? What do you think it means to be "wise"?

----

2. The book of Proverbs is filled with illustrations of how we should live and has much to say on the value of knowledge and wisdom. Read Proverbs 2:1-15. According to verses 1-5, what 7 steps are required before you can gain wisdom?

If you . . .

_____

_____

_____

_____

. . . you will find the knowledge of God.

3. Read verses 7-9. What does God do for those who receive His wisdom?

_____

_____

_____

_____

4. List the results of allowing wisdom to enter your life according to Proverbs 2:10-12.

Verse 10:

1. _____

2. _____

Verse 11:

1. _____

2. _____

Verse 12:

   1._____

   2._____

5. James 3:17 draws a picture of godly wisdom. List the qualities of wisdom that are given in this verse.

_____

_____

_____

_____

6. Who do you know who embodies these traits of wisdom? What is it about them that leads you to this conclusion?

_____

_____

_____

_____

7. If God said to you, "Ask for whatever you want me to give you" (1 Kings 3:5), what would you ask for?

_____

_____

_____

_____

8. Read 1 Kings 3:4-15. What does Solomon request from God?

_____

_____

_____

_____

9. Why does Solomon ask for this?

_____

_____

_____

_____

10. Because God is pleased with Solomon's request, what else does God provide him with?

_____

_____

_____

_____

11. What do the following verses reveal about wisdom?

Psalm 111:10: _____

_____

Proverbs 1:20,29-33: _____

_____

Proverbs 4:1-7: _____

_____

Proverbs 9:9: _____

_____

12. According to Job 28:20-28, where does wisdom come from?

_____

_____

_____

13. Why is the attainment of wisdom so esteemed in the Bible?

_____

_____

_____

_____

14. How can you go about finding God's wisdom?

_____

_____

_____

_____

the gift of knowledge

The biblical gift of knowledge has little or nothing to do with your I.Q. or what grade you received on your last math test or English paper. The spiritual gift of knowledge has been defined as the ability to understand truth that is unknown by natural means.

Open your Bible to 2 Samuel. David is the central figure in the two books of Samuel, but the second book focuses on his life as a leader and king of Israel. David was a great king, but he had his flaws. In 2 Samuel 11, David becomes enamored with Bathsheba, another man's wife, and ends up sending her husband, Uriah, to the front lines of battle, where he is killed. In 2 Samuel 12, we catch up with David in a conversation with the prophet Nathan about his misdoings.

1. Read 2 Samuel 12:1-14. Why does Nathan begin with the tale of the rich man, the poor man and the feast?

2. How does Nathan know of David's sin?

3. How does David respond when he is confronted with the truth about his actions?

4. What is God's purpose in having Nathan confront David?

5. The book of Proverbs contains a great deal of advice about wisdom. Explain the meaning of the following verses.

"Whoever loves discipline loves knowledge, but he who hates correction is stupid" (Proverbs 12:1).

"A prudent man keeps his knowledge to himself, but the heart of fools blurts out folly" (Proverbs 12:23).

"It is not good to have zeal without knowledge, nor to be hasty and miss the way" (Proverbs 19:2).

6. How do you believe the gift of knowledge could be a benefit for the Body of Christ?

reflect

1. How can it be difficult for someone who has the gift of wisdom or knowledge?

_____

_____

_____

_____

_____

2. How might God use the gifts of knowledge or wisdom?

_____

_____

_____

_____

3. Do you believe that you have the gift of wisdom or knowledge? What in particular makes you believe that you have these gifts? Can you remember a time when you believe that you used these particular gifts? Explain.

_____

_____

_____

_____

_____

_____

4. In what areas of your life do you need wisdom right now?

_____

_____

_____

_____

_____

5. What specific ways can you see God using the gift of knowledge in your youth group or in your family?

_____

_____

_____

_____

_____

meditation

For the LORD gives wisdom, and from his mouth
come knowledge and understanding.

PROVERBS 2:6

Answer Key: (1) Trivial Pursuit®; (2) Job, Proverbs, Ecclesiastes, Song of Songs; (3) omniscient; (4) Solomon; (5) sophology; (6) epistemology.

adventurous faith

the gift of faith and
the gift of apostle and missionary

For the LORD gives wisdom, and from his mouth come knowledge and understanding. He holds victory in store for the upright, he is a shield to those whose walk is blameless, for he guards the course of the just and protects the way of his faithful ones.

PROVERBS 2:6-8

While driving home from a rock-climbing trip, a young man named Paul talked about his desire to go to Bible school and become a pastor. For years, Paul had been involved in his church's youth ministry programs, first as a student in his high school ministry and then as part of his church's college ministry team.

Paul's desire to become a pastor wasn't surprising. After all, Paul was a rock climber. He had helped countless students up and down high cliffs, roping them up, preparing them for challenges they had never faced before. Paul was a man of faith—a risk-taker.

A life of faith, risks and adventure was par for his vertical course in life.

Planting a church or ministering to people in a congregation requires a similar great faith, a willingness to take risks, and a radical dependence on God. One of our constant prayers as we work with teenagers should be for God to raise up new leaders for His Church. Like Paul, there are many adventurous young people out there who have the gift of apostle and missionary. We need to encourage them to be bold to use those gifts.

This is the type of lesson where you can instill great challenges of faith and adventure in the hearts of young people. God will use you to plant new visions in open hearts. Who knows . . . you just may have someone like Paul surprise you someday. It's a risk worth taking.

> *Many things are possible for the person who has hope. Even more is possible for the person who has faith. And still more is possible for the person who knows how to love. But everything is possible for the person who practices all three virtues.*
>
> BROTHER LAWRENCE

adventurous faith

the gift of faith and
the gift of apostle and missionary

starter

MISSIONS DISCUSSION: Does your church support missionaries? Do you know who those missionaries are or where they are serving? As a group, locate some information about the missionaries that your church supports and learn about their ministries. Then discuss the following questions:

- What would be fun about being a missionary?

- What would be hard?

- Have you ever met someone with extraordinary faith?

- What about an individual with a remarkable ability for spreading the gospel in other cultures?

Note: You can download this group study guide in 8¹/₂" x 11" format at **www.gospellight.com/uncommon/spiritual_gifts.zip.**

dig

In this study, we will look at two spiritual gifts: the gift of faith and the gift of apostle and missionary.

the gift of faith

"To one is given through the Spirit . . . faith by the same Spirit" (1 Corinthians 12:8-9, *RSV*).

1. Define the word "faith" in your own words.

2. How does Hebrews 11:1 define faith?

All Christians are believers by faith. However, those with the gift of faith have the ability to trust God even in the most extraordinary of circumstances with a deeper level of faith than most of us exhibit. From biblical days to the present day, we can find examples of those who have demonstrated an unusual ability to depend on God.

3. Hebrews 11 is sometimes called the "Faith Hall of Fame."
    This chapter reads like a "Who's Who" list of the faithful.
    Read Hebrews 11. As you read, keep in mind the type of in-
    dividuals on the list and how each demonstrated his or her
    faith. Look back over the verses. For each person listed, de-
    scribe how his or her faith was tested or demonstrated.

    Abel:
    _____
    _____

    Enoch:
    _____
    _____

    Noah:
    _____
    _____

    Abraham:
    _____
    _____

    Jacob:
    _____
    _____

    Moses' parents:
    _____
    _____

    Moses:
    _____
    _____

Israelites ("the people," vv. 29-30):

_____

_____

Rahab:

_____

_____

4. What do you notice about the individuals in this list and the acts of faith they were called to?

_____

_____

_____

_____

_____

5. Do you know any modern-day people who could be included in the "Faith Hall of Fame"? List them below and tell why.

_____

_____

_____

_____

6. Have you ever found it difficult to have faith? When?

_____

_____

_____

_____

7. Read another example of great faith in Luke 7:1-10. Why does the centurion explain to Jesus in verse 8 that he is a man with soldiers under him who obey his commands? What is his point in telling this to Jesus?

_____

_____

_____

_____

_____

8. What happened because of the centurion's faith?

_____

_____

_____

_____

9. Matthew 17 tells a story of Jesus healing a man's son. The man had brought his son to the disciples to be healed, but they were not able to heal the boy. After Jesus restores the boy, the disciples ask Jesus why they weren't able to perform the miracle. What is Jesus' response? (See Matthew 17:20.)

_____

_____

_____

_____

_____

10. Jesus then says, "I tell you the truth, if you have faith as small as a mustard seed, you can say to this mountain, 'Move from

here to there' and it will move. Nothing will be impossible for you" (Matthew 17:20). What is Jesus saying here?

11. What do you think that you could accomplish with your life if you had more faith?

12. What eternal truth is found in Hebrews 11:6?

the gift of apostle and missionary[1]

"His gifts were that some should be apostles" (Ephesians 4:11, *RSV*).

1. Have you ever gone on a missions trip? Where did you go and what did you do?

apostle (n): one sent forth; messenger

To best understand the meaning of apostleship, we must look at the first apostles. They were the commissioned "messengers" of the Early Church. The apostles took the message of the Good News of Jesus Christ to the world. In many ways, they led the way for new territory to be charted for Christ.

A modern-day apostle is one who feels God's call to take the same message of Jesus Christ to the world. Many of these people may work as missionaries. Some people may presume that in order to be an apostle or missionary, you must travel to a distant land, but this isn't true. God may be calling you to be a missionary in your own country, state or city.

In Jesus' time, Paul was one of the most important apostles. In his letter to the Ephesians, he attempts to explain the richness and joy of a life in Christ. Read Ephesians 3:1-13. Go slowly, as it is a wordy passage.

2. What was Paul trying to communicate to the Gentiles? (See Ephesians 3:6.)

   ----

3. What title did Paul give himself? (See verse 7.)

   ----

4. Because of his title, what was Paul able to do? (See verse 8.)

5. What was the goal of his missionary work? (See verses 9-12.)

6. From what you know of Paul, did he accomplish this goal?

7. While some may have a special calling to be apostles or missionaries, as Christians, we are all called by Jesus' Great Commission. Read Matthew 28:16-20. What are we all called to do?

8. What is the importance of having members of the Body of Christ who have the gift of apostle?

_____

_____

_____

_____

_____

9. Do you think you have the gift of apostle or missionary? Why or why not?

_____

_____

_____

_____

_____

10. How would you feel if you sensed that God was calling you to be a missionary?

- ❏   I wouldn't want to go.
- ❏   I'd be nervous.
- ❏   I'd be willing to go if God calls.
- ❏   I'm ready to go today.
- ❏   I'm not the missionary type.
- ❏   I'd be excited about adventure.
- ❏   I'd only want to be a missionary in certain places.

I feel _____

_____ about missionary work.

11. What are the benefits of going on a missions or service trip for you personally?

12. What are the benefits for the people you are serving?

reflect

1. Why is it difficult for some to have complete faith in God?

2. Author and theologian C. S. Lewis once said, "Faith is the art of holding on to things your reason has once accepted in spite of your changing moods." Explain what this means.

3. How are you living a life of faith right now? How are you putting your faith into practice?

_____

_____

_____

_____

_____

4. What areas of your life could use a real "faith lift"?

_____

_____

_____

_____

_____

5. When it comes to being a person with a strong faith in God:

   ❑   I feel very weak. (Read 2 Corinthians 12:9.)
   ❑   I keep trying. (Read Psalm 37:24.)
   ❑   I know God is using me. (Read Philippians 1:6.)

6. What are you doing to be obedient to the Great Commission in Matthew 28?

_____

_____

_____

_____

_____

7. Do you feel that you and the others in your group are inter-
    ested and willing to go on a missions trip? Why or why not?

    _____

    _____

    _____

    _____

8. If you do not have the gift of apostle or missionary, what can
    you do to support the work of Christ around the world?

    _____

    _____

    _____

    _____

meditation

Now faith is being sure of what we hope for and certain
of what we do not see. This is what the ancients were
commended for. And without faith it is impossible to please
God, because anyone who comes to him must believe that
he exists and that he rewards those who earnestly seek him.

HEBREWS 11:1-2,6

Note
1. Some scholars would say that "apostle" and "missionary" are two separate gifts, yet they are
    in the same "gift mix." We have chosen to combine them for the sake of simplicity.

experiencing
God's love

the gift of miracles, the gift of healing, the gift of tongues and the interpretation of tongues

*You are the God who performs miracles; you display
your power among the peoples.*

PSALM 77:14

You may never have seen a blind man healed of his blindness or a lame man walk or a dead person raised from the dead, but if you believe in the God who can perform miracles, you must believe that miracles happen. Why? Because miracles happen every day in teenagers' lives.

Being a youth worker provides all sorts of opportunities to see our awesome God at work. Youth ministry is fertile ground to see the miracles of God take root in the lives of teenagers. It's just that we often forget what miracles really are. How about when a 15-year-old receives Christ for the first time? Isn't that a miracle? What about when a young person overcomes dependency on drugs and alcohol? Isn't that a miracle? What about when a teenager learns to love the parents he used to hate? Now that's a miracle!

Miracles are all around us, but perhaps we've lost our desire to search for signs of God at work in people's lives. Do you still believe in miracles? Do you look for God to demonstrate Himself in amazing and incredible ways?

Miracles are testimonies to the power of God designed to draw us closer to Him. Too often, Christians get split along denominational lines over what constitutes a miracle or what signs and wonders God still performs today. God wants every miracle He performs to bring you closer to Him. Perhaps this lesson will be a reminder to keep looking for signs and wonders in the lives of young people. Young people want to believe in an all-powerful God. Our God is a God of miracles and He uses youth workers like you to show teenagers that both He and miracles still exist.

Let no one therefore say that our Lord Jesus Christ
doeth not those things now, and on this account prefer
the former to the present ages of the Church. . . .
The Lord did those things to invite us to the faith.

St. Augustine

experiencing
God's love

the gift of miracles, the gift of healing, the gift of tongues and the interpretation of tongues

starter

WORD JUMBLE: Unscramble the following words and phrases that are related to spiritual gifts. (Answers can be found at the end of the study.)

1. LIPRUITSA STIFG _____ _____

2. PRATINTEENRITO _____

3. GEHALIN _____

4. FITSG FO SUONTGE _____   _____   _____

5. STIRF SNIORCTANIH _____   _____

Two of the more controversial gifts are the gift of tongues and the interpretation of tongues, and the gift of healing. Both inspire much debate within the Christian Church. We'll take a look at what the Bible has to say about these two spiritual gifts.

dig

the gift of tongues and interpretation of tongues
"To one there is given through the Spirit . . . speaking in different kinds of tongues, and to still another the interpretation of tongues" (1 Corinthians 12:8,10).

In the Christian faith, speaking in tongues and the interpretation of tongues are perhaps the most widely debated and misunderstood gifts of the Spirit. Some say speaking in tongues is not a spiritual gift; others say it is a gift. Some say the gift was only for the first-century Church; others believe tongues to be evidence of the baptism of the Holy Spirit. Let's investigate what the Bible has to say about this interesting gift so that we can begin to develop our own biblical opinion on the subject.

1. Based on what you know, what is the gift of tongues?

_____

_____

_____

_____

It is evident that in the Early Church, many men and women spoke in tongues. The book of Acts, written by Luke, contains the most references to speaking in tongues in the Bible. As Acts begins, we find Jesus' disciples gathered together in the city of Jerusalem during the Pentecost holiday. (Pentecost was a celebration of the anniversary of the giving of the Ten Commandments to Moses at Mount Sinai.) Read Acts 2:1-13.

2. When Moses came face to face with God in the Old Testament, the Bible says that Moses heard a "still, small voice" (1 Kings 19:12, *KJV*). How is the Holy Spirit's arrival described in these verses in Acts?

_____

_____

_____

_____

3. What does the Holy Spirit bring to the disciples?

_____

_____

_____

_____

4. Sometimes people assume that speaking in tongues is gibberish—perhaps divinely inspired, but still nonsense. According to Acts 2, does "gibberish" or "nonsense" describe what the disciples were speaking after the Holy Spirit

came? According to this passage in Acts, what were the disciples saying?

_____

_____

_____

_____

_____

5. How did the people who witnessed this event respond?

_____

_____

_____

_____

_____

6. How would you have responded?

_____

_____

_____

_____

_____

7. Read the following passages. What are some of the circumstances that lead up to people speaking in tongues?

Acts 10:44-46:

_____

_____

_____

Acts 19:1-7:

_____

_____

_____

use

Read 1 Corinthians 14:6-12. Summarize this passage. What is Paul saying about the speaking and interpretation of tongues?

_____

_____

_____

_____

purpose

1. **A sign.** Read 1 Corinthians 14:22 and recall the passage we read from Acts 2. Who is speaking in tongues a sign for?

_____

_____

_____

_____

_____

What is the purpose of the sign?

_____

_____

_____

_____

2. **Edification** (building up the Body of Christ). Read 1 Cor-
    inthians 14:4-5. These verses distinguish between tongues
    and prophecy (interpreted tongues). Who is edified when
    speaking in tongues is interpreted? (Also see verse 26.)

    Who is built up if the tongues are not interpreted?

3. **Prayer.** Read 1 Corinthians 14:14. Do you think speaking in
    tongues is a form of prayer?

biblical guidelines

Paul gave the church at Corinth instructions for speaking in
tongues. He wanted to make it quite clear that the gift of tongues
was no greater than the other gifts of the Spirit. Read 1 Corinthians 14:26-28,33,40 and then list Paul's rules:

1. _____
   _____ (verse 26).

2. _____
   _____ (verse 27).

3. _____
   _____ (verses 27-28).

4. _____
   _____ (verses 33,40).

the gift of healing

"To another gifts of healing by that one Spirit" (1 Corinthians 12:9).

At one time or another, you may have prayed for healing either for yourself or for a loved one. God doesn't always choose to answer these prayers the way we would like, yet we've all heard stories of miraculous healings, unexplained by modern medicine. In addition to the miracles Jesus performed, the Gospels and the book of Acts are filled with examples of God's servants bringing healing and wholeness to those in need.

1. Read the verses below and write down the person who had the gift of healing and what or who they healed. (Note that this is not a complete list.)

PASSAGE	HEALER	WHO/WHAT WAS HEALED
Matthew 8:1-4		
Acts 3:2-8		
Mark 7:31-37		
Acts 8:6-8		
John 5:1-9		
Acts 14:8-10		

These are all examples of physical healing, but it is also possible to experience emotional healing. When Jesus announced the beginning of His ministry in the synagogue in Nazareth, He quoted these words from the prophet Isaiah:

> The Spirit of the Lord is upon me, because he hath anointed me to preach the gospel to the poor; he hath sent me to heal the broken-hearted, to preach deliverance to the captives, and recovering of sight to the blind, to set at liberty them that are bruised (Luke 4:18, *KJV*).

The word translated "broken-hearted" refers to those who are emotionally and mentally shattered. In fact, the last phrase of this quotation, "to set at liberty them that are bruised," also refers to emotional healing.

2. How might someone need emotional healing?

_____

_____

_____

_____

3. What occupations are aimed at providing emotional healing?

_____

_____

_____

4. There is also another form of healing called spiritual healing. Read Matthew 13:14-15. These verses reference a proph-

ecy from Isaiah 6:9-10. How are these verses about Jesus bringing spiritual healing?

5. First Peter 2:24 says, "Christ himself carried our sins on his body to the cross, so that we might die to sin and live for righteousness. By his wounds you have been healed" (*TEV*). According to this verse, why are we healed?

6. How are we healed?

reflect

1. Do the miraculous gifts of healing and tongues have a place in the Church today? Why or why not?

2. Have you ever witnessed someone speaking in tongues or being healed? What was the experience like?

_____

_____

_____

_____

_____

3. How did it impact your faith?

_____

_____

_____

_____

_____

4. Whether or not you have the gift of healing, what can you be doing to help heal people with physical, emotional and spiritual needs?

_____

_____

_____

_____

_____

5. In Matthew 12:38-39, we read that the Pharisees asked Jesus, "Teacher, we want to see a miraculous sign." Jesus rebuked them for asking: "A wicked and adulterous generation asks for a miraculous sign." Yet earlier in Matthew 7, Jesus said,

"Ask and it will be given to you; seek and you will find. . . .
For everyone who asks receives; he who seeks finds" (vv. 7-8).
How can we reconcile these two verses?

_____

_____

_____

_____

_____

6. Is it acceptable to ask for a miracle? Why or why not?

_____

_____

_____

_____

_____

7. What miracles, if any, have taken place in your own life?

_____

_____

_____

_____

_____

_____

8. What miracles would you like to take place in your life?

_____

_____

_____

_____

_____

_____

meditation

You are the God who performs miracles;
you display your power among the peoples.

PSALM 77:14

unit II
spiritual gifts that come alongside God's people

Leonard Bernstein, the famous orchestra conductor, was asked, "What is the most difficult instrument to play?" He responded: "Second fiddle. I can get plenty of first violinists, but to find one who plays *second* violin with as much enthusiasm—that's a problem. And if we have no second fiddle, we have no harmony."

We don't think that the Church has done a good enough job helping students understand that the "come alongside" gifts are just as important to the life of the Church as the "up-front" gifts. This is too bad, because it's very exciting for the kid in your group who is an incredible encourager but not a very good teacher of the Word to see that he or she is also grace gifted.

These "come alongside" gifts are the backbone of the Church. Many who have this gift mix do not receive the pats on the back or the words of encouragement that they should from church leadership. Well, that is about to change! We hope you will encourage like crazy your kids who have some of these serving gifts.

encouraging God's people

the gift of exhortation

May our Lord Jesus Christ himself and God our Father, who loved us and by his grace gave us eternal encouragement and good hope, encourage your hearts and strengthen you in every good deed and word.

2 THESSALONIANS 2:16-17

In the bottom drawer of the blue file cabinet that sits next to my desk, I have a whole file filled with scraps of paper, scrawled notes, greeting cards, personal stationery and notebook paper. *All letters of encouragement and thanks.* This isn't a "How Great I Am" file, but a file full of thanksgiving and honest appreciation. It's the type of file every youth worker needs to encourage him or her when life and ministry look hopeless.

In your work with teenagers, who is your encourager? Who is your Barnabas? Discouragement is one of the major diseases of youth ministry. It's so easy for a youth worker to be discouraged by "getting dissed" . . .

- *Dis*respect: You spend three hours working on a talk and when you try to deliver it, nobody is listening. They're all talking and joking around.

- *Dis*appointment: You hear rumors that one of your key leadership students is making some big-time mistakes. When you try to talk to him, he flat-out lies to your face. What do you do—call him a liar?

- *Dis*interest: Your youth ministry borders on the double-edged razor of apathy and boredom. You've tried everything, but you're now ready to give up.

- *Dis*illusionment: You thought youth ministry would be fun and exciting, but you're seeing no evidence of teenagers walking closer with God.

The devil would love to do you in with discouragement, but today the Holy Spirit wants to empower you with encouragement. Let this lesson be an affirmation of His work in your life and a reminder that He's still in control.

All of us need encouragement—somebody to believe in us.
To reassure and reinforce us. To help us pick up the pieces and go on.
To provide us with increased determination in spite of the odds.
CHARLES SWINDOLL

encouraging
God's people

the gift of exhortation

starter

WHAT'S THE DIFFERENCE? What is the difference between a friend and a truly good friend? Think about the qualities that separate those truly special to us.

A friend <u>lends a hand if it's convenient</u>, but a *good* friend

_____.

A friend <u>tells you what you want to hear</u>, but a *good* friend

_____.

A friend _____, but a *good* friend

_____.

Note: You can download this group study guide in 8^1/$_2$" x 11" format at **www.gospellight.com/uncommon/spiritual_gifts.zip.**

A friend _____, but a *good* friend

_____ .

A friend _____, but a *good* friend

_____ .

dig

We have different gifts, according to the grace given us . . .
if it is encouraging, let him encourage.
ROMANS 12:6,8

The word "exhortation" means "to come alongside." When you exhort someone, you come alongside that person to encourage and support him or her. You've probably been around people who have a real gift for encouraging others. They have the unique ability to make you feel special. Their ministry of comfort, challenge and counsel helps and heals discouraged people.

1. Who is someone in your life who provides advice and encouragement to you?

_____

_____

_____

2. What qualities or characteristics are helpful for someone with the gift of exhortation to have?

_____

_____

_____

3. The apostle Paul had the gift of exhortation. As you read the
   book of Acts, you will see that Paul was an encouragement
   to others even though he himself suffered great trials, en-
   during brutal beatings, mobs and imprisonment. How did
   Paul use his gift of exhortation in these Scripture passages?

   Acts 14:21-22

   _____

   _____

   Acts 20:17-35

   _____

   _____

4. Read 1 Corinthians 9:19-23. How does Paul relate to the
   people he is preaching to?

   _____

   _____

   _____

   _____

5. Read 1 Corinthians 1:4-9 and Philippians 4:13. What com-
   pliments does Paul give the church at Corinth? Of what
   strength does he remind the Philippians?

   _____

   _____

   _____

   _____

6. Read Philippians 1:6 and 2 Corinthians 4:8-10,16-17. What hope does Paul give the Philippians? What reminder of hope does he give the Corinthians?

    _____

    _____

    _____

7. Read Galatians 4:8-20 and 1 Thessalonians 4:2-8. What is Paul's difficult message to the Galatians? What hard truth does Paul give to the Thessalonians?

    _____

    _____

    _____

8. Another New Testament Christian who stands out as possessing the gift of exhortation is Barnabas. Everywhere Barnabas appears in the Bible, he is encouraging someone. According to Acts 4:36, what does "Barnabas" mean?

    _____

    _____

    _____

9. Read Acts 11:19-26 and list several ways Barnabas was an encouragement to the believers in Antioch.

    _____

    _____

    _____

Although Barnabas and Paul were great champions for the faith, they didn't always get along. Acts 13 tells how Barnabas and Paul left the church in Antioch and began to preach around the world. On their first long trip, they took Barnabas's nephew John (called Mark), who Barnabas saw as a potential Christian leader. (Barnabas saw and encouraged potential in people.) John Mark didn't make it through the entire trip, leaving to return to Jerusalem (see Acts 13:13).

After the first trip was completed, Paul and Barnabas decided to go back to visit the churches they had planted (see Acts 15:36). Barnabas wanted to take John Mark along again, but Paul insisted that because John Mark had deserted them on their earlier trip, they should not take him. A sharp disagreement broke out. Paul's priority was their work; Barnabas's priority was people (see Acts 15:37-41).

10. Read Acts 15:36-41. What was the result of their argument? (See verses 39-40.)

_____

_____

_____

_____

11. If you were Paul, would you have given John Mark a second chance? Why or why not?

_____

_____

_____

12. What characteristics made Barnabas a good friend?

_____

_____

_____

_____

We might be missing a big chunk of the Bible had Barnabas not used his gift of encouragement. Although Barnabas never wrote a book in the New Testament, Paul wrote 13 and Mark wrote 1— and Barnabas encouraged them both!

reflect

1. Who in your life needs your encouragement?

_____

_____

_____

_____

2. What specifically can you do to encourage him or her?

_____

_____

_____

_____

3. Encouragement isn't only done with words. What other ways could you demonstrate your encouragement for someone?

_____

_____

_____

4. Why is it important to have people who encourage us, especially in our walk with Jesus?

5. Why is it sometimes difficult to encourage others?

6. The gift of exhortation involves encouragement and occasional confrontation. Why is it difficult to confront someone even though you know it will help him or her get back on the right path?

7. Have you ever had to confront a friend with a difficult truth in order to help him or her get back on track? What was the result?

meditation

Let us not give up meeting together, as some are
in the habit of doing, but let us encourage one another—
and all the more as you see the Day approaching.

HEBREWS 10:25

session 6

giving it away

the gift of giving

But just as you excel in everything—in faith, in speech,
in knowledge, in complete earnestness and in your love for us—
see that you also excel in this grace of giving.

2 CORINTHIANS 8:7

Many young people in the church have not been taught the importance of giving. Not being eager to part with what little cash they have, they don't know what a great privilege giving is. Youth pastors rarely talk about it. Very few sermons explain it so that kids can understand. All they know is that when the basket is passed, they're "supposed" to throw in a couple bucks.

We cheat our students when we neglect to teach them the grace of giving. We've all seen this principle at work in other peoples' lives. A father who didn't attend the church where his boys were involved in the youth group is a great example. Every so often, he'd call the youth pastor and ask, "What kinds of needs do you have in your youth ministry?" A few days later, the youth group would receive a check in the mail to invest in the lives of young people. This dad knew how to excel in the grace of giving. He blessed countless lives by giving to others what God had given to him.

Giving is a wonderful way to free yourself from the trappings of materialism and the desire to hoard riches. Giving, not only monetarily but also of your time and talents, is one of the most practical, spiritual investments you can ever make. When you teach young people to be cheerful, generous givers, you are equipping them to understand how to be a good steward of all God has given them. You also help them to receive the wonderful blessings God pours out to those who trust Him with everything.

We don't suddenly, someday, have an abundance of time and money to give. We begin with the little pieces. We are in training now, learning bit by bit to manage money, power, time, relationships and temptation. Then maybe someday we will find ourselves competent to manage life on a grander scale.

LYNN ANDERSON

giving it away

the gift of giving

starter

GIFTS DISCUSSION: As a group, discuss the following questions:

- What is one of the best gifts that you have ever received?
- What is one of the best gifts that you have ever given?

dig

If it is contributing to the needs of others, let him give generously.

ROMANS 12:8

The gift of giving is a special ability that God gives to certain members of the Body of Christ to generously and cheerfully contribute their time, talent and treasures to the work of the Lord.

Note: You can download this group study guide in 8¹/₂" x 11" format at **www.gospellight.com/uncommon/spiritual_gifts.zip.**

1. What is an example of giving your time?

2. What is an example of giving your talent?

3. What is an example of giving your treasure?

the macedonians' example

Paul explains the gift this way: "And since we have gifts that differ according to the grace given to us, let each exercise them accordingly . . . he who gives, with liberality" (Romans 12:6,8 *NASB*). Another translation says, "If God has given you money, be generous" (Romans 12:8, *TLB*). In his second letter to the Corinthians, Paul highlights an example of giving by the Macedonian church. Read 2 Corinthians 8:1-7.

1. Was it easy for the Macedonian church to give? Why or why not?

2. How much did they give?

3. According to verse 4, what was the Macedonians' attitude toward giving?

4. Why do you suppose Paul is telling the church of Corinth about the Macedonians? (See verses 10-12.)

becoming better givers

Although some individuals have specifically received the spiritual gift of giving from the Holy Spirit, we all are called to be cheerful givers. How can we become better givers?

give without boasting

Read Matthew 6:1-4. Why do you think we should give in secret?

_____

_____

_____

_____

give with a proper perspective

Read 1 Timothy 6:10. This often-misquoted passage doesn't say "money is the root of all evil" but "the love of money is a root of all kinds of evil." What is the danger of loving money? How can loving money impact your giving?

_____

_____

_____

_____

give sacrificially

Read Mark 12:41-44. Why was the widow honored more than the rich people? What lesson can we apply from this story to our own giving?

_____

_____

_____

_____

give what you have
Read Luke 12:48. What does Jesus mean when He says, "From everyone who has been given much, much will be demanded"?

_____

_____

_____

_____

give without comparison
Read 2 Corinthians 9:7-8. How much is the "right amount" for a person to give? What is God's promise to the giver?

_____

_____

_____

_____

reflect

1. Is giving part of your spiritual life? Why or why not?

_____

_____

_____

_____

2. How can you become a better giver?

_____

_____

_____

_____

3. Is it easier for you to give of your time, talent or treasure? Which is the hardest? Why?

    _____

    _____

    _____

    _____

    _____

4. Why is it foolish to be selfish with our time, money or talent? (Read 2 Timothy 6:7.)

    _____

    _____

    _____

    _____

5. Read 1 Timothy 6:17-19. What does this passage indicate that God requires of a rich person?

    _____

    _____

    _____

    _____

6. Do you think God gives mainly rich people the gift of giving? Why do you think so?

    _____

    _____

    _____

    _____

7. Why might it be easier for those with little to give big?

8. Who is someone who you could bless through giving in this next week? How specifically can you bless them?

9. Acts 20:35 includes the familiar saying that "It is more blessed to give than to receive." What is the meaning of this simple yet profound statement?

10. Describe a time when you were blessed by giving to someone else. Do you think you were more blessed than the person to whom you gave?

11. Why do you think God wants us to give?

_____

_____

_____

_____

_____

meditation

But just as you excel in everything—in faith, in speech,
in knowledge, in complete earnestness and in your love
for us—see that you also excel in this grace of giving.

2 CORINTHIANS 8:7

taking time to care

the gift of serving and
the gift of helping

Be shepherds of God's flock that is under your care, serving as
overseers—not because you must, but because you are willing, as God
wants you to be; not greedy for money, but eager to serve.

1 PETER 5:2

Most youth workers know that youth ministry isn't the place to look for applause, standing ovations and visits to the Oval Office. Much of youth ministry happens through the secret, invisible work of volunteer youth workers who just may be someone like you.

Countless volunteers help out teenagers in incredible ways that most people never even think of and with little applause or attention. Like Mary, who scrubs out pots of dry, crusted spaghetti in the camp kitchen. Or Jim, who keeps the youth bus in good running condition at no charge. Or Pete, who faithfully gets up at 6:00

A.M. on Sunday mornings to mop a bandroom floor covered with sticky wrappers, spilled Coke and muddy grass so that teenagers have a clean place to sit on Sunday morning. Add to Mary, Jim and Peter the long parade of volunteers who have spent numerous late-night hours counseling students, surviving 10-hour bus rides and sleeping in the dirt during Mexico missions trips.

These people are heroes. These people really care.

Most youth workers, in one way or another, have the spiritual gifts of serving and helping. You can see it in the ways they meet the unique needs of teenagers. You can see it in their attitudes and in their smiles. By helping young people be all that God has de-signed them to be, youth workers model a selfless, others-centered way of living. That's living the life of Christ in full color.

If you are serving and helping young people in the name of Je-sus Christ, you can bet He's getting a standing ovation in heaven. That's what giving glory to God is all about. Keep up the good work.

When Christ calls a man, He bids him come and die.

DIETRICH BONHOEFFER

taking time to care

the gift of serving and
the gift of helping

starter

FLASHBACK: Has someone ever gone out of their way to help and serve you? It might be a teacher who stayed all afternoon helping you work on an essay, a waiter who made your visit to a restaurant special, or a friend who gave up their own time to help you. Think back and share a time when someone went above and beyond to serve you.

dig

Throughout the Bible, we see Christians being called to serve and help those around them. Christians are still called to do the same

Note: You can download this group study guide in 8½" x 11" format at www.gospellight.com/uncommon/spiritual_gifts.zip.

today. But we don't have to do it on our own; the Holy Spirit gives individuals the spiritual gifts of serving and helping.

the gift of serving

"We have different gifts, according to the grace given us . . . Let [each] use it in proportion to his faith. If it is serving, let him serve" (Romans 12:6-7).

1.   What are some jobs in our society that are based on serving?

-----------------------------------   -----------------------------------

-----------------------------------   -----------------------------------

-----------------------------------   -----------------------------------

-----------------------------------   -----------------------------------

-----------------------------------   -----------------------------------

The life of Jesus provides us with an example of the perfect servant. While some expected Jesus to come as a boisterous warrior with a large, showy army, Jesus instead came humbly to show us how to love and serve. "If anyone wants to be first, he must be the very last, and the servant of all," Jesus told His disciples (Mark 9:35).

2.   Read John 13:1-20. In these verses, we read that Jesus is about to have dinner with His disciples when He does something unusual. What are the two reasons that Jesus washes the disciples' feet? (See verses 1 and 15.)

----

3. Why does Peter say he doesn't want Jesus to wash his feet?

4. Jesus replies to Peter by saying, "Unless I wash you, you have no part with me" (v. 8). Explain Jesus' response.

5. Being a servant is not always easy or fun, even for those who have the gift of serving. Yet in spite of the difficulties and sacrifices, we all are called to be servants. According to the following verses, why should we persevere in servanthood despite the difficulties?

1 Peter 2:21-24

Matthew 25:35-40

6. Read Galatians 5:13-15. According to these verses, if we love and serve one another, what will we prevent?

    _____

    _____

    _____

    _____

7. Read Matthew 19:30. How does this verse relate to the quote about being second fiddle? What does Jesus mean when He says the "last shall be first"?

    _____

    _____

    _____

    _____

the gift of helping

"And in the church God has appointed . . . those able to help others" (1 Corinthians 12:28). The gift of helping is the special ability to assist others to increase their effectiveness in life. The person with the gift of helping is often a background person who makes things happen without being noticed. Even though this gift is often overlooked, it is a vital act of ministry in the Church.

1. Do you know people with the gift of helping? Who are they, and what do they do?

    _____

    _____

    _____

In Paul's letters, he often mentions "faithful helpers." These helpers were apparently the backbone of the Early Church. These faithful helpers freed up Paul and the other leaders to do mighty works of ministry. Without the helpers, there would have been no Pauls or Peters in the Early Church.

2. How did the following individuals act as helpers for the apostles and the Early Church?

Priscilla and Aquila (Read Romans 16:3-6.)

_____

_____

_____

Tryphena, Tryphosa and Persis (Read Romans 16:12.)

_____

_____

_____

Epaphroditus (Read Philippians 2:25-30.)

_____

_____

_____

3. What attitudes or qualities do you feel that a person with the gift of helping needs to have?

_____

_____

_____

_____

4. Which of these attitudes and qualities do you possess?

_____

_____

_____

_____

_____

5. Which do you struggle with?

_____

_____

_____

_____

_____

6. Read Philippians 2:3-11. How does Paul suggest we help others, according to verses 3 and 4?

_____

_____

_____

_____

_____

7. What is the central theme of verses 5 through 8?

_____

_____

_____

8. What is the result of Christ's obedience and service, according to verses 9 though 11?

reflect

1. Why should we serve others?

2. After working through this session, what are some of the "thankless" jobs you now have a better appreciation for at church and at home?

3. List some ways you can work at being a servant in the following areas:

At home:

At school:

_____

_____

At church:

_____

_____

4. What specific areas of your life need to change so that you can be more of a servant?

_____

_____

_____

_____

5. How can serving others benefit you?

_____

_____

_____

_____

6. Think of someone in your life who acts as a servant. What is one thing you could do for them this week to thank them for all that they do?

_____

_____

_____

meditation

Whatever you do, work at it with all your heart,
as working for the Lord, not for men, since you know that
you will receive an inheritance from the Lord as a reward.
It is the Lord Christ you are serving.

COLOSSIANS 3:22-24

the open heart

the gift of mercy and the gift of hospitality

Here I am! I stand at the door and knock. If anyone
hears my voice and opens the door, I will come in
and eat with him, and he with me.

REVELATION 3:20

For many veteran youth workers, meals shared with young people over the years prove to be among their fondest memories. Breakfast, lunch, dinner, late night snacks—they've sat around the table with students at all hours of the day and night. If they've been working with youth for a while, they may play host to mid-20s newlyweds whom they've known since they were freshmen in high school! It is a wonderful privilege to see God's continued work in their lives, and often, some of these "former" students become very special friends.

As we grow in our relationship with Jesus, He wants us to become closer and closer friends with Him. He wants to take us to new depths in our understanding of who He is and how we can know Him better. Every day, He wants us to invite Him into our homes. Jesus wants to sit down and chat. He wants to share a meal with us. The message of Revelation 3:20 is that we have the opportunity to show hospitality to Jesus every day.

How can you keep Jesus locked out of your heart? By being too busy! Your schedule as a youth worker can be very demanding, but it will never be able to compete with the deep joy and satisfaction that come from meeting with God every day. As you study the spiritual gifts of mercy and hospitality, may you be refreshed by the mercy of God and, in response, renew your desire to meet with Jesus today. He is knocking on the door of your heart, waiting for you to invite Him in. Before opening your door to students, open your heart to Jesus first.

It's only by His mercy that we are not destroyed totally and completely. Therefore, we should be imitators of God and show mercy to those God brings our way.

ELLIOT JOHNSON/AL SCHIERBAUM

the open heart

the gift of mercy and the gift of hospitality

starter

CHECKLIST. Look at the list below and check off those issues that you feel most passionate about.

- ☐ homelessness
- ☐ the persecuted Church
- ☐ battered women
- ☐ literacy
- ☐ poverty
- ☐ the environment
- ☐ endangered animals
- ☐ gun violence
- ☐ the elderly

- ☐ HIV/AIDS
- ☐ teen pregnancy
- ☐ bullying
- ☐ hunger
- ☐ child abuse
- ☐ drug and alcohol abuse
- ☐ gangs
- ☐ violence in schools
- ☐ depression

- ❐ the developmentally disabled   ❐ the physically handicapped
- ❐ war   ❐ living wage

There are so many needs in the world that it can be overwhelming. But it is valuable to keep this saying by Helen Keller in mind: "I am only one, but I am still one. I cannot do everything, but I can still do something." What are *you* doing?

dig

Mercy and hospitality are two of the spiritual gifts discussed in Romans. As with many of the spiritual gifts, these gifts have to do with how we treat and interact with others.

1. How would you define mercy?

_____

_____

_____

_____

_____

2. How would you define hospitality?

_____

_____

_____

_____

_____

the gift of mercy

"And since we have gifts that differ according to the grace given to us, let each exercise them accordingly . . . he who shows mercy, with cheerfulness" (Romans 12:6,8 *NASB*).

The gift of mercy is a gift that gets little recognition yet has great personal rewards. To have mercy means to be kind or compassionate, and to relieve suffering, to forgive. The gift of mercy may be demonstrated by direct personal involvement with the sick, outcast, poor, aged, mentally ill, deformed, hungry, shut-in, disabled, deprived, widowed, sad, underprivileged, alcoholic or drug-addicted. A person with the gift of mercy understands and fervently wants to meet the needs of those who hurt.

The Pharisees and other masters of the Old Testament Law were always trying to test Jesus by scrutinizing His words and actions. In the following passage from Luke, Jesus talks about loving your neighbor. One of the teachers asks who we ought to consider our neighbor. Read Luke 10:30-37 to see Jesus' response.

1. You may recognize this story as the parable of the Good Samaritan. What acts of mercy did the Samaritan perform?

This man not only felt sorry—he *acted!* He went further than feeling sympathy and went out of his way to help.

2. Read Matthew 18:21-35. In this passage, Peter asks Jesus
    how many times he should forgive someone who sins
    against him. Jesus says that he should forgive 77 times. Are
    we really supposed to forgive someone exactly 77 times?
    What is Jesus' point here?

    ----

2. How does Jesus' parable in this passage relate to our rela-
    tionship with God?

    ----

3. Are there certain groups that you feel are easier to be mer-
    ciful to? Are there certain groups to whom it is more diffi-
    cult to show mercy? Explain these answers.

    ----

4. What do you think are the areas of greatest need in your particular community?

_____

_____

_____

_____

_____

5. What are the areas of greatest need in the world?

_____

_____

_____

_____

_____

_____

6. Do you struggle with showing mercy? Fill in the blanks in the following verses to learn some keys to developing your empathy and mercy.

For all have _____ and fall short of the _____ of God (Romans 3:23).

Do not _____ , or you too will be _____ . Why do you look at the _____ of sawdust in your brother's eye and pay no attention to the _____ in your own eye? (Matthew 7:1,3).

But when the _____ and _____
of God our Savior appeared, he saved us, not because of
_____ things we had done, but because of his
_____ (Titus 3:4-5).

Once you were not a people, but now you are the _____
of God; once you had not received _____,
but now you have received _____
(1 Peter 2:10).

Be _____ and _____ to one another, for-
giving each other, just as in Christ God _____ you (Ephesians 4:32).

What does the LORD require of you? To act _____
and to love _____ and to walk _____ with
your God (Micah 6:8).

Administer true _____; show _____ and
_____ to one another. Do not
_____ the widow or the fatherless, the alien
or the poor. In your hearts do not think evil of each other
(Zechariah 7:8-10).

the gift of hospitality

"Practice hospitality" (Romans 12:13, *RSV*). If you enjoy organiz-
ing and hosting a party, making newcomers to a group feel welcome or sharing with those in need, you may have the gift of
hospitality. Hospitality is demonstrating kindness in welcoming
guests or strangers, and it requires finding ways to put others at
ease and meet their needs.

1. Describe a time when someone made you feel comfortable or welcome in a new situation.

   ....

   ....

   ....

   ....

2. Read Luke 7:36-50. This story is about faith and forgiveness but also about hospitality. Even though it is not the woman's house, how does she demonstrate hospitality to Jesus?

   ....

   ....

   ....

   ....

3. Why is it ironic that the Pharisee is upset that the woman is being hospitable to Jesus?

   ....

   ....

   ....

4. Read Matthew 25:34-40. According to these verses, why should we be generous with our hospitality?

   ....

   ....

   ....

   ....

In the days of Jesus and the Early Church, people were dependent on others for food and lodging as they traveled from city to city. When Jesus was preparing to send out His disciples on their first mission trip, He gave them these instructions: "Don't take any money in your money belts—no gold, silver, or even copper coins. Don't carry a traveler's bag with a change of clothes and sandals or even a walking stick. Don't hesitate to accept hospitality, because those who work deserve to be fed" (Matthew 10:5,9-10).

5. Do you think there is still a need for the gift of hospitality today with all the restaurants, motels and hotels that are available to travelers? Explain your thoughts.

6. Look up the verses below and list the name of the person who was hospitable and what he or she did to show hospitality.

Acts 9:43

Acts 16:15

Acts 16:34

7. What are some examples of how the gift of hospitality can be used in the Church?

8. How can you demonstrate hospitality in your own life?

9. Read 1 Peter 4:9. Why do you think Paul adds "ungrudgingly" (*RSV*) or "without grumbling" (*NIV*) when he speaks of being hospitable?

reflect

1. You may have heard the saying, "Grace is getting what we don't deserve, and mercy is not getting what we do deserve." Has someone ever shown you mercy? Explain.

_____

_____

_____

_____

_____

_____

2. Describe a time when someone showed hospitality to you. How did it make you feel?

_____

_____

_____

_____

_____

3. God calls us to be merciful and hospitable even if these are not our spiritual gifts. What steps can you take to work on developing mercy and hospitality?

_____

_____

_____

_____

_____

4. Read James 2:14-17. How are showing hospitality and mercy an important part of our faith in Jesus?

5. Who in your community needs your mercy and hospitality? How can you welcome them and meet their needs?

meditation

I tell you the truth, whatever you did for one of the least
of these brothers of mine, you did for me.

MATTHEW 25:40

unit III

spiritual gifts that provide communication and leadership

When Doug was in tenth grade, I asked him to prepare a brief sermonette for a Youth Sunday program at our church. I love Youth Sundays, but as you know, the messages are usually strong with the heart and weak with the presentation.

Doug stood before our congregation wearing a tie. He said, "Jim Burns and my parents asked me to dress up for my first sermon. I'm wearing a tie. Now that they have seen it on me . . ."

He took off his clip-on tie, placed it on the pulpit and gave the best Youth Sunday message I have heard to this day. Our pastor leaned over to me and said, "I think that young man is after my job!" From that day on, I knew Doug had the spiritual gift of pastor/teacher. My job as his youth worker was to affirm his giftedness and give him lots of opportunity to use his gifts.

You have students with pastoral abilities and other communication gifts. Your job is to help them understand those gifts and give them every opportunity to use them to the glory of God.

sharing the good news

the gift of evangelism and the gift of prophecy

How beautiful on the mountains are the feet of those who bring
good news, who proclaim peace, who bring good tidings, who proclaim
salvation, who say to Zion, "Your God reigns!"

ISAIAH 52:7

Tom is a contagious Christian. In high school, he was heavily involved in the party scene and only came to youth group a few times. But during college, he finally became a Christian—and his enthusiasm for Jesus hasn't died down yet! Whether at home, work, school or on the volleyball court, Tom is always looking for new ways to share the Good News of Jesus Christ. Tom is a perfect example of what being an evangelist is all about.

One of the greatest myths in Christendom today is that you have to be the next Billy Graham in order to tell someone about

Jesus. The devil would love to discourage all believers by having us compare ourselves to Billy Graham or someone like Tom. A lot of young people, including many youth workers, are flat out scared about sharing their faith. They're not very good evangelists and they know it.

If you or someone you know feels like this, it's important to remember that God doesn't keep a scorecard. He wants to free you of your fears of telling people about Him. And most of all, He doesn't want you to spend endless amounts of wasted time comparing yourself to others. Hopefully, this lesson will help you to look at evangelism and prophesy in a new light. You may not be a great evangelist, but remember that the Body of Christ isn't just a mouth, is it?

The gospel is not theology. It's a Person. Theology doesn't save.
Jesus Christ saves. The first-century disciples were totally involved with
a Person. They were followers of Jesus. They were learners of Jesus.
They were committed to Jesus. They were filled with Jesus.

RICHARD HALVERSON

sharing the good news

the gift of evangelism and the gift of prophecy

starter

WHAT IF? As a group, have the members discuss how their lives would change if . . .

. . . they were an only child.

. . . they lost the ability to speak.

. . . it was illegal to be a Christian.

. . . they had to move to a foreign country.

. . . they could see into the future.

. . . all cell phones stopped working.

. . . they could live to be 150 years old.

. . . their parents became missionaries.

dig

Evangelism and prophecy are both spiritual gifts that have to do with speaking. Those with the gift of evangelism are gifted at spreading the news about Jesus' life, death and resurrection, while those with prophetic abilities are able to warn people about the consequences when they are headed in the wrong direction.

the gift of evangelism

"He gave some to be . . . evangelists" (Ephesians 4:11).

The word "evangelist" appears only three times in the entire New Testament (see Acts 21:8, Ephesians 4:11 and 2 Timothy 4:5). Although the word isn't used many times, its meaning is clearly defined: "one who proclaims the Good News." While the gift of evangelism and the gift of the apostle (see session 3) are often related, they do have some differences. The gift of evangelism is the ability to share the Good News of salvation through Jesus, whereas the gift of apostle allows individuals to go forth and cross cultural boundaries to establish churches, overcome differences and teach about Jesus.

1. Read Matthew 28:16-20. This passage has often been called "The Great Commission." Jesus had been crucified and three days later had risen from the dead. He called His disciples together on a mountaintop in Galilee. Why do you think this passage is called "The Great Commission"?

    _____

    _____

    _____

2. Why are there only 11 disciples with Jesus at this point? (See Matthew 27.)

3. Verse 17 reads, "When they saw [Jesus], they worshiped him; but some doubted." These are the disciples, some of Jesus' closest followers and yet even some of them doubted. What comfort can this verse give to us?

4. Look closely at the verbs in verses 19-20. What are the disciples asked to do? List just the verbs here.

   Verse 19:

   Verse 20:

5. What do you notice about these verbs?

The Great Commission is a call to action. These verses do not say, "Sit at home and pray" or "Join a committee to plan an outreach." Jesus' first command? *Go.*

Yet evangelism is not always easy, even for those with the spiritual gift of evangelism. Thankfully, God gives us help.

6. Read Acts 1:8. According to this verse, who empowers us to go and share the Good News?

7. The Bible tells us that Philip was an evangelist (see Acts 21:8). Read Acts 8:4-8 and describe the actions of Philip and the actions of the crowd.

8. In Acts 8:12, what message is Philip spreading?

The job of an evangelist is not to nurture Christians but rather to preach to unbelievers the message of salvation in Christ.

the gift of prophecy

"But one who prophesies, preaching the messages of God, is help-ing others grow in the Lord, encouraging and comforting them" (1 Corinthians 14:3, *TLB*).

When we hear the word "prophet," we often think of someone who can predict the future. That is indeed one way God uses prophets—as foretellers of things to come—but He also uses peo-ple with the gift of prophecy as *"forth*-tellers," from the Greek meaning "to speak forth" or "to proclaim." As forth-tellers, proph-ets have the role of proclaiming God's truth, pointing out the sin in people's lives and warning them about the consequences of their actions. *— lonely occupation*

John the Baptist is one example of a prophet who warned peo-ple about the consequences of their sinfulness. Read the account of John the Baptist in Luke 3:2-18.

1. According to Luke's reference to the prophet Isaiah, what was John the Baptist's job?

   _____

   _____

   _____

2. In verses 10-18, what kind of advice and wisdom did he give to the people?

   _____

   _____

   _____

3. What did John the Baptist explain was the difference be-
    tween him and Jesus?

    _____

    _____

    _____

    _____

    _____

4. What are the roles of the prophet? Read the following pas-
    sages of Scripture to determine the various jobs of those
    with the gift of prophecy:

    Deuteronomy 18:17-19

    _____

    _____

    _____

    1 Corinthians 14:3

    _____

    _____

    _____

    Jeremiah 46:1; 47:1; 48:1; 50:1

    _____

    _____

    _____

5. Paul stresses the importance of the gift of prophecy in
    1 Corinthians 14:1-5,39. Read these verses. Why do you
    think Paul views prophecy as being so important?

6. What issues do you think a person with the gift of proph-
    ecy would speak on in the present day?

7. Do you know someone who has the gift of prophecy? If so,
    how does he or she make you feel when you hear him or
    her speak?

reflect

1. Why is sharing our faith a scary experience sometimes?

   _____
   _____
   _____
   _____

2. What hinders you from sharing the Good News?

   _____
   _____
   _____
   _____

3. Have you ever shared your faith with someone who wasn't a believer? Describe the experience.

   _____
   _____
   _____
   _____

4. Do you think we still have prophets today? Who?

   _____
   _____
   _____
   _____

Who do you know who has the gift of evangelism? How do you know?

5. How can you tell if a prophet is from God?

_____

_____

_____

_____

6. Church growth experts estimate that 25 percent of people would come to church if you asked. With the Great Commission in mind, who are two people you could invite to church next week?

_____

_____

_____

_____

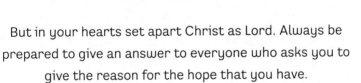

meditation

But in your hearts set apart Christ as Lord. Always be
prepared to give an answer to everyone who asks you to
give the reason for the hope that you have.

1 Peter 3:15

building up the church

the gift of teaching and the gift of pastoring

*And the things you have heard me say in the presence
of many witnesses entrust to reliable men who will also be
qualified to teach others.*

2 TIMOTHY 2:2

Write down the five most influential sermons you've ever heard.

Hard, isn't it?

Okay, now write down the five most influential people in your life.

Doesn't take long, does it?

The point is simple and obvious: People remember people; they rarely remember words. Though you may spend hours on messages or lesson preparation, it's critical to remember that your students will remember you more than your words. Teaching is important, but your role as a pastor to your students puts your life and teaching in perspective. Your students don't want you to inspire them so much as they want you to encourage and listen to them. They want to know that you care about them.

You are influencing the Church of Jesus Christ for today and the next generation. Never forget that. Do you want students to remember your words or your life? Which will they remember? Do you really care if they remember that Bible study on Babylonian license plate numbers? Teaching and learning the Word of God is very important, but remembering a life is much easier than remembering someone's words. How many sermons can you remember?

If you are not a disciple-maker, then I would suggest that you do the same thing that Timothy did with Paul, or that Peter, James, and John did with the Lord Jesus. Make yourself available to a disciple-maker who can help you to become a disciple-maker.

WALTER HENRICHSEN

building up the church

the gift of teaching and
the gift of pastoring

starter

STUPID HUMAN TRICKS: Know how to wolf whistle, cartwheel or drink through your nose? Choose a few members to teach their skill to the rest of the group.

dig

Teachers. Coaches. Bosses. Family. Pastors. Who are the people in your life who have taught you the most? Those with the gift of teaching or pastoring have the unique ability to guide and inform us, but they are also in the position to have a great influence on our confidence, outlook and goals.

Note: You can download this group study guide in 8$\frac{1}{2}$" x 11" format at www.gospellight.com/uncommon/spiritual_gifts.zip.

the gift of teaching

"So we are to use our different gifts in accordance with the grace that God has given us . . . If it is to teach, we must teach" (Romans 12:6-7, *TEV*).

There are some teachers who have a remarkable impact on our lives. Usually it is not so much what they teach as how they teach. These teachers have a special gift to make spiritual truth and other subjects come alive. Many of these teachers use their gift to greatly influence our lives.

1. Think about the different kinds of teachers you have had in your life. Who is a teacher who . . .

Taught you a new skill? What skill did he or she teach you?

_____

_____

_____

_____

Taught you facts or information? What facts/information?

_____

_____

_____

_____

Taught you something about life? What life lesson?

_____

_____

_____

_____

Taught you about faith in Jesus? What faith lesson?

2. Teaching does not come easy to many people. Which two of the following would be the hardest for you to teach?

- ☐ someone older than you
- ☐ someone younger than you
- ☐ someone how to play a sport
- ☐ someone how to play an instrument
- ☐ someone how to get from point A to point B
- ☐ your parents
- ☐ your grandparents
- ☐ a stranger
- ☐ a close friend
- ☐ someone who speaks a different language

3. Why would you find this so hard?

Even if we don't have the gift of teaching, we will all likely come across opportunities when we are required to provide instruction to others. How can we learn to be better teachers? By learning from Jesus' example.

sorts of gift of teaching

4. *Jesus earned the respect of His students.* Read Matthew 7:28-29 and Mark 1:22. How did Jesus earn the respect of His audience in this passage?

    _____

    _____

    _____

    _____

    _____

5. *Jesus was humble about His knowledge.* In John 8:28, according to Jesus, who deserved the credit for His knowledge?

    _____

    _____

    _____

    _____

    _____

6. *Jesus taught with compassion.* According to Mark 6:33-34, why did Jesus stop to teach the people?

    _____

    _____

    _____

    _____

    _____

7. *Jesus spoke plainly and in ways that the people understood.* Read Mark 4:30-34. Why did Jesus rely on parables to teach?

_____

_____

_____

_____

_____

8. *Jesus fervently sought after knowledge and wisdom.* According to the story told in Luke 2:45-47, where did Jesus' parents finally find Him?

_____

_____

_____

_____

_____

9. *Jesus taught truth, even when it was hard for the people to hear.* Read John 6:53-64. What message was hard for the disciples to hear in this passage?

_____

_____

_____

_____

_____

10. According to the Bible, those with the gift of teaching are held by a higher standard than others. Read James 3:1. Why might teachers be judged more harshly than others?

the gift of pastoring

"And his gifts were that some should be . . . pastors" (Ephesians 4:11, *RSV*). "Pastor" is the Latin word for *shepherd*. Those with the gift of pastoring are charged with guiding others in the ways of the Lord. It's not just a spiritual gift for the pastor of your church. You may have this gift, too.

1. Read John 10:11-16. What qualities of a shepherd are described in this parable from Jesus?

2. What would a shepherd of people, instead of sheep, do?

3. Use each passage to discover a role of a shepherd.

PASSAGE	ROLE OF A SHEPHERD
Matthew 9:36	
Matthew 25:32	
John 10:11	
John 10:14	
Luke 15:2-6	

Can you see how the New Testament portrays the shepherd as the person who cares for the flock and leads them into safe places? If the sheep wander away, the shepherd seeks them out and saves them. He or she protects them from their enemies.

4. Besides the pastor of your church, who is someone else you know with the gift of pastoring? How does he or she demonstrate their gift?

5. How can you "pastor" your friends? List three friends and some specific action you could take to shepherd, pastor and care for each of them this week.

NAME OF FRIEND   HOW YOU CAN SHEPHERD THIS WEEK

reflect

1. What qualities make someone a good teacher, regardless of what he or she is teaching?

2. Beyond preaching sermons and performing weddings and funerals, what new roles do you understand that a pastor of a church is responsible for?

_____

_____

_____

_____

3. Why might the gifts of teaching and pastoring make those who have them more vulnerable to pride or a focus on self?

_____

_____

_____

_____

4. Why might pastors and teachers be especially in need of encouragement?

_____

_____

_____

_____

5. Think about an important teacher and/or pastor in your life. What could you do to encourage and thank him or her this week?

_____

_____

_____

_____

meditation

Don't let anyone look down on you because you are
young, but set an example for the believers in speech,
in life, in love, in faith and in purity. . . . devote yourself
to the public reading of Scripture, to preaching
and to teaching. Do not neglect your gift, which was
given you through a prophetic message when the body
of elders laid their hands on you.

1 TIMOTHY 4:12-14

knowing where to go

the gift of leadership and
the gift of administration

Not everyone who says to me, "Lord, Lord," will enter the
kingdom of heaven, but only he who does the will of my
Father who is in heaven. Many will say to me on that day,
"Lord, Lord, did we not prophesy in your name, and in your
name drive out demons and perform many miracles?"

MATTHEW 7:21-22

If you have spent any time in the super-sized bookstores lately, you will notice that the leadership and business management sections are booming. Every day, more and more books come out on leadership development, leadership strategy, empowerment, re-engineering and personal success. However, if you take the message of some of these books and then compare them to God's plan for leadership development found in the Bible, you'll see some crucial differences:

POPULAR BOOKS SAY:	GOD SAYS:
"Be powerful!"	"Be humble."
"Take charge!"	"Submit."
"Be in control!"	"Give up control."
"Rule with an iron fist."	"Serve in love."
"Win at all costs!"	"Count the cost."

Jesus Christ asks His followers to walk with Him in a completely different style of leadership and obedience. God wants you to administer His kingdom—not the kingdom of man. Leadership without an authentic love for God is hollow. Christian leadership without servanthood is hypocrisy.

Most people don't want to be led, but they are willing to be served. You have the opportunity to show students a different way: the way of God. The way of the Cross. Students will eagerly walk with an honest, authentic person who serves others before themselves. You can show your students Jesus' design for following Him. Use this lesson to explore how you can be servant leaders of Jesus in order to administer His kingdom here on Earth.

He who cannot obey, cannot command.

BENJAMIN FRANKLIN

knowing where to go

the gift of leadership and
the gift of administration

starter

KNOW YOUR LEADERS: How well do you know your leaders? See how many of the following questions you can answer.

- What is the name of the current president?

- What is the name of the current vice-president?

- What is the name of the Secretary of Defense?

- What is the name of your state's U.S. senators?

- What is the name of your state governor?

- What is the name of your city mayor?

Note: You can download this group study guide in 8¹/₂" x 11" format at
www.gospellight.com/uncommon/spiritual_gifts.zip.

dig

What qualities make someone a good leader? What traits make someone gifted at administration? Do leaders need to love the limelight? Must administrators thrive on paperwork? In this study we will look at these two related spiritual gifts.

the gift of leadership

"And since we have gifts that differ according to the grace given to us, let each exercise them accordingly . . . he who leads, with diligence" (Romans 12:6,8, *NASB*).

Many times when we hear the word "leader," we think of an authority figure standing above everyone else, directing people in the way they should go. You may think of a leader as someone who has an outgoing personality or the ability to speak well in front of groups. But these qualities do not always make a person a good leader. Even if you are shy and timid, you may have real leadership ability. Perhaps you are a leader but you've never realized it!

1. Think back over the various leaders you have encountered in your life. Who was one leader that stands out in your mind as exemplary? Why? What made him or her memorable and worthy of your attention?

The literal definition of a leader is one who "stands before" others. This means that the gift of leadership is the special ability from God to set goals and then lead others to work together to carry out those goals for the glory of God.

To help shatter some of our misconceptions about what it means to be a leader, let's take a look at Timothy. Timothy was a follower of Jesus who frequently traveled with the apostle Paul on his missionary journeys. At a young age, Timothy took over the leadership of the church of Ephesus at Paul's request.

Although this young man was not particularly experienced, Paul saw leadership qualities within Timothy that let him know he would be capable of such a task. In Philippians 2, Paul says about Timothy, "I have no one else like him . . . [he] has proved himself, because as a son with his father he has served with me in the work of the gospel" (vv. 20,22).

2. In Paul's letters to Timothy, he writes to encourage Timothy in his task. Read the following verses from Paul's letters. After each verse, find the advice that Paul gives to Timothy concerning leadership.

1 Timothy 4:12

13-15
1 Timothy 6:14

----

2 Timothy 2:22-26

2 Timothy 4:6-7

3. Jesus Christ gives us a perfect model of leadership. From what you know of the life of Jesus, can you recall specific times when Jesus used the gift of leadership?

Jesus appointed, trained and led 12 apostles who, after His death, became the leaders of the Early Church (see Acts 4:37; 9:27). During Christ's time with these apostles, He taught them many things, including leadership.

4. According to Mark 10, two of Christ's apostles, James and John, asked Him an interesting question. Read Mark 10:35-41. What was their question?

5. Why do you think they asked this question? What was their motivation?

6. Let's see how Jesus responded to their question. Read Mark 10:42-45. What point is Jesus trying to make in these verses?

7. What should the words "leader" and "servant" mean to a Christian?

8. How does this differ from how the world views these roles?

the gift of administration

"God has appointed in the church . . . administrators" (1 Corinthians 12:28, *RSV*). The gift of administration is very similar to the gift of leadership. The difference is that leadership is defined by what a person *is*, while administration is defined by what he or she *does*.

The Greek word Paul used that is translated "administrators" refers to a helmsman or pilot (captain) who steers a ship through rocks and sandbars to safe harbor. The gift of administration is the special ability that God gives to certain members of the Body of Christ that helps them to clearly understand the present and future goals of a group.

1. People with the gift of administration are able to plan workable ways to reach these goals. How does this differ from the gift of leadership?

    _____

    _____

    _____

    _____

    _____

    _____

Open up the Old Testament to Exodus 18. In this chapter in the Bible, we read that Moses and the Israelites have escaped from their slavery in Egypt and are on their way to the land of Canaan. Jethro, a priest and Moses' father-in-law, visits Moses and gives him some valuable advice to aid his ministry to the Israelites. Read Exodus 18:13-27.

2. What was the problem that Jethro foresaw with the way Moses was running things?

3. What advice did Jethro give to Moses?

4. How did this advice affect the life and work of Moses?

5. How does this passage demonstrate Jethro's gift of administration and not a gift of leadership?

6. How could someone with this gift benefit . . .

Your youth group?

_____

_____

_____

_____

_____

Your church?

_____

_____

_____

_____

7. Can a leader also have the gift of administration? Explain.

_____

_____

_____

_____

8. What positive steps should the leader take if he or she doesn't have the gift of administration?

_____

_____

_____

_____

_____

reflect

1. What should you do if you sense or are told you have leadership or administrative abilities, but are also timid and shy?

2. Why is it that we often do not associate the term "leader" with "servant"?

3. How can we put into practice Jesus' command that "whoever wants to be great among you must be your servant" (Mark 10:43)?

4. In what ways was Jesus a leader to His disciples?

5. In what way was He a leader to the crowds?

6. In what way was He a leader to His enemies?

7. Leaders and administrators have a lot of responsibility. How can you pray for the leaders and administrators in your youth group, church, family, school, community and world?

meditation

Remember your leaders, who spoke the word of God to you.
Consider the outcome of their way of life and imitate their faith.

HEBREWS 11:7

spritual gifts
discovery

Not that we are competent in ourselves to claim anything for ourselves,
but our competence comes from God. He has made us competent
as ministers of a new covenant—not of the letter but of the Spirit;
for the letter kills, but the Spirit gives life.

2 CORINTHIANS 3:5-6

As you close this study on spiritual gifts, don't forget the greatest spiritual gift of all: Jesus Christ. Jesus has first and foremost called you to a growing, deepening relationship with Him. He hasn't called you to a spectacular program that draws hundreds of teenagers, a concert series, a Bible study or a lock-in. He hasn't even called you to be the greatest youth worker in the world. Or even the greatest youth worker in Pokamoko, Missouri.

God doesn't want you to depend on your spiritual gifts, talents, skills, passions, personality, looks or unique ability to perform stupid youth worker tricks. God has called you to depend on Him. If you have a tendency to forget this, be thankful that we have a God full of mercy, grace, forgiveness and every other spiritual gift imaginable. His heart's desire is for us to depend on Him. With the spiritual gifts and blessings He's given us, He wants to work through our lives for His purpose.

Being dependent on God is a great way to show your love and appreciation for Him. As you depend on Him in every situation you encounter, you will model to your students a life devoted to God. What students want and need most is to see God at work in your life. They don't want to see your spiritual gifts as much as they want to see God in action.

Before you begin this lesson on discovering your spiritual gifts, why not spend some time with the greatest spiritual gift of all?

God has also designed the gifts to help "unite" the body of Christ . . . thus the gifts of the Spirit should never divide the body of Christ; they should unify it.

BILLY GRAHAM

spritual gifts
discovery

You can offer the following spiritual gifts assessment to your whole group. Have them take the inventory during your group meeting or class, or distribute the student handouts at the end of session 11 and ask them to complete the inventory before session 12. If you take the second option, have the students bring their completed assessments with them to session 12, and lead a discussion about what they discovered. Consider grouping students with similar gifting in pairs or smaller groups to deepen the dialogue. Encourage them to take a second look at the previous sessions in this study that explore their particular gifts.

Note: You can download this group study guide in 8$^1/_2$" x 11" format at **www.gospellight.com/uncommon/spiritual_gifts.zip.**

spiritual gifts inventory

Step 1: Go through the following list of 120 statements and think about how each one applies to you. For each statement, mark on the answer sheet on page 169 how true each statement is of your life: MUCH, SOME, LITTLE or NOT AT ALL.

Step 2: Follow the instructions given on the answer sheet to score your gifts inventory.

1. I could be described as an "others-centered" person.
2. I believe I have the gift of helping.
3. I enjoy giving hope to those in need.
4. When people are in need I enjoy having them in my home. I do not feel like they are intruding.
5. I believe I have a prayer language that is in a tongue unknown to me.
6. God has used me in a supernatural way to heal someone.
7. I believe I have the gift of exhortation.
8. I see myself as a person who is very generous when it comes to giving money to my church.
9. My friends view me as a person who is wise.
10. I have expressed thoughts of truth that have given insight to others.
11. I often feel I know God's will even when others aren't sure.
12. I would like to be a missionary.

13. I can tell nonbelievers about my relationship with Christ in a comfortable manner.

14. I have given others important messages that I felt came from God at the perfect time.

15. I enjoy explaining biblical truths to people.

16. I have a way of relating to and comforting those who have fallen away from the Lord.

17. I believe I know where I am going, and other people seem to follow.

18. I see clearly that a job can be done more effectively if I allow others to assist.

19. Many incredible acts of God have happened to others through me.

20. There has been a time when I heard someone speak in an unknown language and I was able to interpret what he or she said.

21. I enjoy meeting the needs of others.

22. I'm the one who often cleans up after the meeting without being asked.

23. I believe I have the gift of mercy.

24. I enjoy having strangers in my home. I like making them feel comfortable.

25. I have spoken in tongues.

26. I have healed a physically disabled person.

27. I believe I have the ability to comfort those who are "off-track" and help them get back on track.

28. I believe I have the gift of giving.

29. I believe that God has given me the ability to make wise decisions.

30. I desire fully to understand biblical truths.

31. I enjoy helping others with spiritual needs.

32. I feel comfortable when I'm around people of a different culture, race or language.

33. I believe I have the gift of evangelism.

34. I believe I have the ability to reveal God's truth about the future.

35. I think I have what it takes to teach a Bible study or lead a small-group discussion.

36. I try to know people in a personal way so that we feel comfortable with one another.

37. I would enjoy leading, inspiring and motivating others to become involved in God's work.

38. I would enjoy directing a vacation Bible school, recreation program or special event for my church.

39. God has used me to specifically perform miraculous signs and wonders.

40. I believe I have the gift of interpretation of tongues.

41. You'll frequently find me volunteering my time to help with the needs of the church.

42. I seldom think twice before doing a task that might not bring me praise.

43. I would like to visit rest homes and other institutions where people need visitors.

44. I believe I have the gift of hospitality.

45. When I speak in tongues, I feel God's Spirit within me.

46. The gift of healing is evident in my life.

47. I have a desire to learn more about counseling so that I can help others.

48. I have a strong desire to use my money wisely, knowing God will direct my giving.

49. I believe God has blessed me with the gift of wisdom.

50. I am able to help others understand God's Word.

51. I find it easy to trust in God in difficult situations.

52. I adapt easily to a change of setting.

53. I have the ability to direct conversations toward the message of Christ.

54. I believe I have the gift of prophecy.

55. I am willing to spend extra time studying biblical principles in order to communicate them clearly to others.

56. I would like the responsibilities that my pastor has.

57. I want to lead people to the best solution when they have troubles.

58. I can give others responsibilities for a task or project and help them accomplish them.

59. God has performed humanly impossible miracles through my life.

60. God has shown me what someone is saying when he or she is speaking in tongues.

61. I'm the type of person that likes to reach out to less fortunate people.

62. I receive joy doing jobs that others see as "thankless."

63. I am very compassionate to those in need.

64. I believe God has given me the ability to make others feel comfortable in my home.

65. I believe I have the gift of tongues.

66. I have the ability to heal.

67. I have helped others in their struggles.

68. I am confident that God will take care of my needs when I give sacrificially and cheerfully.

69. I feel confident that my decisions are in harmony with God's will.

70. I believe I have the gift of knowledge.

71. I trust in God for supernatural miracles.

72. I have a strong desire to see people in other countries won to the Lord.
73. I have led others to a personal relationship with Christ.
74. I have had the chance to proclaim God's truth at the required time.
75. I believe I have the gift of teaching.
76. I would like to be a pastor.
77. I have influenced others to complete a task or to find a biblical answer that helped their lives.
78. I am able to set goals and plan the most effective way to reach them.
79. Others have mentioned to me that I was used by God to bring about a supernatural change in their lives.
80. I have been used to interpret tongues, and Christ was glorified as a result.
81. I feel good when I help with the routine jobs at the church.
82. I am able to do jobs that others won't do and I feel good about myself.
83. I have a desire to work with people who have special physical needs.
84. I want my house to always be a spot where people in need can come and find rest.
85. An unknown language comes to me when I'm at a loss for words in my prayer time.
86. God is glorified when He heals others through me.
87. I enjoy seeing people respond to encouragement.
88. I am a cheerful giver of my money.
89. I usually see clear solutions to complicated problems.
90. I have the ability to learn new insights on my own.
91. I believe I have the gift of faith.

92. I am willing to go wherever God wants to send me.
93. I desire to learn more about God so that I can share Him in a clearer way.
94. I have given messages that were judgments from God.
95. Others tell me I present the gospel in a way that is easy to understand.
96. When I teach from the Bible, my concern is that I see results in the spiritual growth of others.
97. I believe I have leadership skills.
98. I enjoy learning about management issues and how organizations function.
99. I have witnessed God's miraculous power in and through my life.
100. I have interpreted tongues in such a way that it has blessed others.
101. I believe I have the gift of serving.
102. You'll often find me volunteering to do "behind the scenes" activities that few notice but that must be done.
103. I would like to have a ministry with those who are needy.
104. I enjoy providing food and housing to those in need.
105. Others have interpreted my unknown prayer language.
106. I believe I have the gift of healing.
107. I am known for the way I encourage others.
108. I enjoy giving money to the needy.
109. God has given me the ability to give clear counsel and advice to others.
110. I tend to use biblical insights when I share with others.
111. Others in my group see me as a faithful Christian.
112. I believe I could learn a new language well enough to minister to those in a different culture.

113. I always think of new ways in which I can share Christ with my non-Christian friends.

114. I desire to speak messages from God that will challenge people to change.

115. Because of my teaching, I have brought others to a better understanding of the Christian faith.

116. I can see myself taking responsibility for the spiritual growth of others.

117. When I'm in a group, I'm usually the leader or I take the lead if no one else does.

118. I believe I have the gift of administration.

119. I believe I have the gift of miracles.

120. God has used my gift of interpretation of tongues to speak a message to the church.

answer sheet

In the grid on page 170, enter the numerical value of your response beside the number of the corresponding statement from the Spiritual Gifts Inventory. (Note that the grid runs top to bottom, not left to right, so make sure that you enter your answer for item 2 below your answer for item 1.)

When you have completed the gifts inventory, add across each row and place the sum in the "Total" column. Circle your top three scores, then look at the gifts list at the bottom of the page. Each gift corresponds to one of the lettered rows above. You can fill in all the blanks in the "Gift" column, or just fill in your top three.

Now that you have a better idea of what your spiritual gifts may be, review what you have learned in the previous sessions about how best to use them!

MUCH=3   SOME=2   LITTLE=1   NOT AT ALL=0

	ANSWERS						TOTAL	GIFT
A	1.___	21.___	41.___	61.___	81.___	101.___		
B	2.___	22.___	42.___	62.___	82.___	102.___		
C	3.___	23.___	43.___	63.___	83.___	103.___		
D	4.___	24.___	44.___	64.___	84.___	104.___		
E	5.___	25.___	45.___	65.___	85.___	105.___		
F	6.___	26.___	46.___	66.___	86.___	106.___		
G	7.___	27.___	47.___	67.___	87.___	107.___		
H	8.___	28.___	48.___	68.___	88.___	108.___		
I	9.___	29.___	49.___	69.___	89.___	109.___		
J	10.___	30.___	50.___	70.___	90.___	110.___		
K	11.___	31.___	51.___	71.___	91.___	111.___		
L	12.___	32.___	52.___	72.___	92.___	112.___		
M	13.___	33.___	53.___	73.___	93.___	113.___		
N	14.___	34.___	54.___	74.___	94.___	114.___		
O	15.___	35.___	55.___	75.___	95.___	115.___		
P	16.___	36.___	56.___	76.___	96.___	116.___		
Q	17.___	37.___	57.___	77.___	97.___	117.___		
R	18.___	38.___	58.___	78.___	98.___	118.___		
S	19.___	39.___	59.___	79.___	99.___	119.___		
T	20.___	40.___	60.___	80.___	100.___	120.___		

A. Serving
B. Helping
C. Mercy
D. Hospitality
E. Tongues
F. Healing
G. Exhortation
H. Giving
I. Wisdom
J. Knowledge
K. Faith
L. Apostle and Missionary
M. Evangelism
N. Prophecy
O. Teaching
P. Pastoring
Q. Leadership
R. Administration
S. Miracles
T. Interpretation of Tongues

HOME**HW**WORD

Get Equipped with HomeWord...

LISTEN
HomeWord Radio
programs reach over 800 communities nationwide with *HomeWord with Jim Burns* – a daily ½ hour interview feature, *HomeWord Snapshots* – a daily 1 minute family drama, and *HomeWord this Week* – a ½ hour weekend edition of the daily program, and our one-hour program.

CLICK
HomeWord.com
provides advice and resources to millions of visitors each year. A truly interactive website, HomeWord.com provides access to parent newsletter, Q&As, online broadcasts, tip sheets, our online store and more.

READ
HomeWord Resources
parent newsletters, equip families and Churches worldwide with practical Q&As, online broadcasts, tip sheets, our online store and more. Many of these resources are also packaged digitally to meet the needs of today's busy parents.

ATTEND
HomeWord Events
Understanding Your Teenager, Building Healthy Morals & Values, Generation 2 Generation and Refreshing Your Marriage are held in over 100 communities nationwide each year. HomeWord events educate and encourage parents while providing answers to life's most pressing parenting and family questions.

A Ministry with *Jim Burns*

In response to the overwhelming needs of parents and families, Jim Burns founded HomeWord in 1985. HomeWord, a Christian organization, equips and encourages parents, families, and churches worldwide.

Find Out More
Sign up for our FREE daily e-devotional and parent e-newsletter at HomeWord.com, or call 800.397.9725.

HomeWord.com

Small Group Curriculum Kits

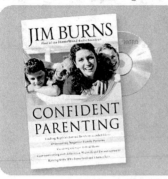

Confident Parenting Kit

This is a must-have resource for today's family! Let Jim Burns help you to tackle overcrowded lives, negative family patterns, while creating a grace-filled home and raising kids who love God and themselves.

Kit contains:
- 6 sessions on DVD featuring Dr. Jim Burns
- CD with reproducible small group leader's guide and participant guides
- poster, bulletin insert, and more

Creating an Intimate Marriage Kit

Dr. Jim Burns wants every couple to experience a marriage filled with A.W.E.: affection, warmth, and encouragement. He shows husbands and wives how to make their marriage a priority as they discover ways to repair the past, communicate and resolve conflict, refresh their marriage spiritually, and more!

Kit contains:
- 6 sessions on DVD featuring Dr. Jim Burns
- CD with reproducible small group leader's guide and participant guides
- poster, bulletin insert, and more

Parenting Teenagers for Positive Results

This popular resource is designed for small groups and Sunday schools. The DVD features real family situations played out in humorous family vignettes followed by words of wisdom by youth and family expert, Jim Burns, Ph.D.

Kit contains:
- 6 sessions on DVD featuring Dr. Jim Burns
- CD with reproducible small group leader's guide and participant guides
- poster, bulletin insert, and more

Teaching Your Children Healthy Sexuality Kit

Trusted family authority Dr. Jim Burns outlines a simple and practical guide for parents on how to develop in their children a healthy perspective regarding their bodies and sexuality. Promotes godly values about sex and relationships.

Kit contains:
- 6 sessions on DVD featuring Dr. Jim Burns
- CD with reproducible small group leader's guide and participant guides
- poster, bulletin insert, and more

Parent and Family Resources from HomeWord
for you and your kids...

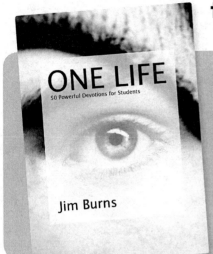

One Life Kit

Your kids only have one life – help them discover the greatest adventure life has to offer! 50 fresh devotional readings that cover many of the major issues of life and faith your kids are wrestling with such as sex, family relationships, trusting God, worry, fatigue and daily surrender. And it's perfect for you and your kids to do together!

Addicted to God Kit

Is your kids' time absorbed by MySpace, text messaging and hanging out at the mall? This devotional will challenge them to adopt thankfulness, make the most of their days and never settle for mediocrity! Fifty days in the Scripture is bound to change your kids' lives forever.

Devotions on the Run Kit

These devotionals are short, simple, and spiritual. They will encourage you to take action in your walk with God. Each study stays in your heart throughout the day, providing direction and clarity when it is most needed.

90 Days Through the New Testament Kit

Downloadable devotional. Author Jim Burns put together a Bible study devotional program for himself to follow, one that would take him through the New Testament in three months. His simple plan was so powerful that he was called to share it with others. A top seller!

Tons of helpful resources for youth workers, parents and youth. Visit our online store at www.HomeWord.com or call us at 800-397-9725

Small Group Curriculum Kits

Confirming Your Faith Kit

Rite-of-Passage curriculum empowers youth to make wise decisions...to choose Christ. Help them take ownership of their faith! Lead them to do this by experiencing a vital Christian lifestyle.

Kit contains:
- 13 engaging lessons
- Ideas for retreats and special Celebration
- Solid foundational Bible concepts
- 1 leaders guide and 6 student journals (booklets)

10 Building Blocks Kit

Learn to live, laugh, love, and play together as a family. When you learn the 10 essential principles for creating a happy, close-knit household, you'll discover a family that shines with love for God and one another! Use this curriculum to help equip families in your church.

Kit contains:
- 10 sessions on DVD featuring Dr. Jim Burns
- CD with reproducible small group leader's guide and participant guides
- poster and bulletin insert
- 10 Building Blocks book

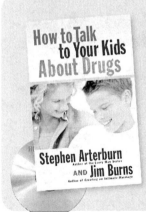

How to Talk to Your Kids About Drugs Kit

Dr. Jim Burns speaks to parents about the important topic of talking to their kids about drugs. You'll find everything you need to help parents learn and implement a plan for drug-proofing their kids.

Kit contains:
- 2 session DVD featuring family expert Dr. Jim Burns
- CD with reproducible small group leader's guide and participant guides
- poster, bulletin insert, and more
- How to Talk to Your Kids About Drugs book

Tons of helpful resources for youth workers, parents and youth. Visit our online store at www.HomeWord.com or call us at 800-397-9725

uncommon high school
resources for leaders

The Christian Life
ISBN 0-8307-4644-7
ISBN 978-0-8307-4644-6

The Life of Jesus
ISBN 0-8307-4726-5
ISBN 978-0-8307-4726-9

Resisting Temptation
ISBN 0-8307-4789-3
ISBN 978-0-8307-4789-4

Parents & Family
ISBN 0-8307-5097-5
ISBN 978-0-8307-5097-9

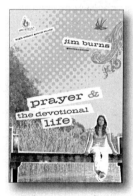

Prayer & Worship
ISBN 0-8307-5479-2
ISBN 978-0-8307-5479-3

The New Testament
ISBN 0-8307-5566-7
ISBN 978-0-8307-5566-0

The Old Testament
ISBN 0-8307-5645-0
ISBN 978-0-8307-5645-2

**Sharing Your Faith
& Serving Others**
ISBN 0-8307-5714-7
ISBN 978-0-8307-5714-5

Winning Spiritual Battles
ISBN 0-8307-5836-4
ISBN 978-0-8307-5836-4

uncommon
leaders' resources

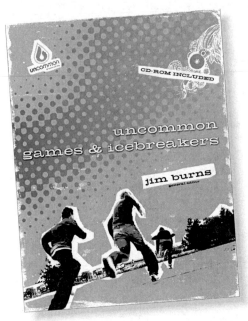

uncommon games
and icebreakers

Jim Burns, General Editor
Manual w/ CD-ROM
ISBN 978.08307.46354

uncommon Bible
study outlines
and messages

Jim Burns, General Editor
Manual w/ CD-ROM
ISBN 978.08307.46330